FINDING MONEY FOR YOUR SMALL BUSINESS

By: Kris Solie-Johnson

American Institute of Small Business
426 Second Street
Excelsior, MN 55331
952-545-7001
Fax: 952-545-7020
www.aisb.biz   info@aisb.biz

Copyright 2007

Published by: American Institute of Small Business
426 Second Street
Excelsior, MN 55331
952-545-7001

Printed in the United States of America

Solie-Johnson, Kris.
    Finding money for your small business / by Kris Solie-Johnson
    p. cm.
    Includes index.
    ISBN 978-0-939069-14-8
1. Small business – Finance. 2. Entrepreneurship
I.   Title.

Table of Contents

Preface

Finding Money for Your Small Business is a step-by-step guide to help you get the money you need to start up or fuel up your small business. It is written so it can be easily understood, even by people who have no previous business experience. Of course, you may discover some words and ideas that are new to you, but I've tried to explain them in the simplest way possible.

As a hands-on teaching kit *Finding Money for Your Small Business* will show you things to do and things not to do in your search for financing. It will give you real answers to real questions. I've tried to make it a clear and easy-to-understand reference that covers every aspect of finding where the money is and how to use other people's money to arrive at the success you're seeking.

Small business owners usually go into business with knowledge of certain areas and a tremendous lack of information and insight in other areas. Small business owners can't afford the kinds of help available to larger businesses. This book will supply a major part of the financing help you'll need, but there will be times when you will need specialized help, and I'll show you where to get it - sometimes for free.

One problem that faces new and established companies is that of determining true financial needs. Don't think that the more money a company has, the better. Good companies can fail if they have too little money to meet day-to-day costs. A good company can also run into trouble if it has too much financing. The secret is to find the level that will ensure proper operations without burdening your company with too much debt repayment.

Some people make the mistake of finding out how much money is available, then justifying that amount with what is needed to start or run the company. That's why this book goes into some detail about the steps you must follow to avoid that trap, such as:

- Forecasting sales and estimating cost of goods sold and operating expenses.
- Preparing a list of all the equipment your company needs to purchase in order to operate efficiently.
- Estimating expenses for starting a new business or expanding your existing business.
- Preparing a projected income statement.

You'll learn how to convert the projected income statement, startup expenses, and equipment purchases to a cash flow statement that will tell you how much money you need to for efficient, profitable operation of your company.

Then, when you have determined how much money your company needs, I'll indicate what sources are available and how this money can be obtained. In most new companies without enough financial history to prove their ability to repay loans, it is difficult to borrow from traditional sources. I also have provided a description of non-traditional sources for those of you who need to take a more creative approach.

Whatever the source, you will be able to borrow only the amount for which you can demonstrate an ability to repay and for which you can provide adequate collateral to protect the lender. Previous years' financial information plus the projected income statements and projected cash flow statements will help you accomplish that task. In general, lending institutions are willing to lend an amount that can be repaid by your company's income and cash flow.

Are you prepared to lose your savings for the sake of your business? If not, you should probably question your confidence in the venture and your commitment to it. Would you decide against starting up if you knew your chances of staying in business for two years were less than fifty-fifty? These are the actual odds for success and failure in a new business. But not every business starts with the same odds. Those businesses started by people with business experience and expertise have a far greater chance of success, while those started by owners with little or no experience or expertise have a far greater chance of failing.

Like any book, Finding Money for Your Small Business can't do more for you than you are ready and willing to do for yourself. Starting or making more of your own small business requires three things:

1. The desire to take charge of your own future.
2. The willingness to work hard.
3. A practical understanding of how to do the work and organize for success.

Do you have a positive attitude? With all the ups and downs in the business world, an optimistic outlook is a necessity. You have to be able to view each setback as a stepping stone to your eventual success.

Do you plan ahead? Probably the most important ability necessary for business success is planning. Going into business with detailed plans increases the likelihood of business success.

Can you take advice from others? Nobody knows it all or has the time or money to make every mistake on his or her own. Being open to the wisdom and experience of others is the hallmark of a leader. People who listen spend more time doing what works, and less time doing what doesn't.

I have seen small business success happen hundreds of time before. People who have a good idea and a good attitude, and who are willing to act on good advice, have made it in small business. You can do it, too, and I'm here to show you how to get the money that is the lifeblood of all business.

Chapter 1

Getting Started

So you want to start your own business. Or, you have a business that is "starved" for money, either to keep it operating or to take it to the next level of success. You've learned, or you will soon, that the basic ingredient of any successful business is having proper financing to survive and prosper.

The problem is as simple as this: You open your business, but before the first customer hands over the first dollar, you have to pay your rent, phone bills, and you have to buy inventory and fixtures. You need funds for living expenses and salaries. It all takes money that you either have already or that you'll have to go out and get. It's the basic challenge every businessperson has to face, not just at the start, but again and again for as long as he or she stays in business.

That's what this book is all about: how to get the money to get going and keep going. This book will show you what it takes to start a small business. You will answer some tough questions about you and your competition to arrive at a frank answer about whether you should even go into business for yourself and what your chances for success will be. The next step will be to decide whether you should start a new business, buy one that's already operating or maybe buy a franchise.

You will determine how much money will you need to not only start your business but also keep it up and running? *Finding Money for Your Small Business* is intended to get you started on the road to finding the basic sources of money that you should be considering. It covers the difference between equity and debt

1

financing and the kinds of loans that are available from banks. Other sources of money to consider include commercial finance companies, venture capital funds, life insurance companies, government, your home, lease financing, trade credit foundations and pension funds.

Equally important, you will get some pointers on how to approach lenders and what you'll have to do to convince them you're a good risk. By the time you finish reading this book, you should have a firm idea of where to find the right money that meets your business needs and your goals.

IF YOU ALREADY OWN A SMALL BUSINESS

As a small business owner you don't have to be reminded of the money difficulties that can arise, usually at the most unexpected times. You know all the costs of operating a business, such as:

▪ Salaries	▪ Rent
▪ Materials	▪ Taxes
▪ Technology	▪ Interest on loans
▪ Advertising	▪ Professional services
▪ Insurance	▪ Working capital
▪ Utilities	▪ Miscellaneous Costs

There are always demands on your bank accounts, and if income doesn't meet them you have to find someone who can help you.

Something like this may have happened to you or someone you know: Tom Reilly is a successful businessman who has a well-established mail order business. For years he has depended on a weekly mailbox full of checks to pay the twice-monthly salaries for his five employees and himself. One Monday the mail was unexpectedly light, and the checks he expected are nowhere in sight. If he doesn't take some fast action, he'll have to dig into his savings or get the money elsewhere

2

to meet the payroll. Fortunately, Tom had built up a good relationship with his banker over the eight years he had been in business. He pays a visit to the bank and, because of his established good record, got a loan on the spot.

Any kind of business, new or established is in constant need of money. If sales keep up and customers pay their bills, things run smoothly. There are also times when sales keep growing, customers keep paying, but they are not paying as fast as you need to pay your bills. This is a cash flow shortage.

IF YOU ARE STARTING A SMALL BUSINESS

When starting a new business, there are three important factors to consider: the idea, the need/want for your product or service, and the type of competitors you will face.

The Idea

Every business venture is based on an idea. If your idea involves a product, will you manufacture, subcontract, assemble or buy it? Will it be more suitable for retail or mail order? Does it require a sales staff or distributors? If it is a new product, will you need a model, patent, or copyright? If it's an existing product, what makes your product better than all other options?

If your idea is for a service, can it be handled by you or will it require other personnel? Are special skills or equipment, or both, required? If you don't have the skills, are they available through employees? Can the service be organized and marketed? Is it a new service or an improvement of an existing service?
If your idea is for a retail establishment, will it be something new or competitive? Will location be its primary asset? What will set it apart from other retailers? Will the adjacent stores create the type of traffic you desire?

The Need

Is there a real need for what you have to offer? Does a market exist, and is it

3

reasonably large enough for you to enter? Will there be opportunity for future growth? Where are the buyers who need your product or service - in industry or in the consumer marketplace? Are there any other restrictions to your market: age, disposable income level, geography, or season? Will you have to create a market? How do you know the market wants your product/service? Can you prove it? Is the market easy and cost effective to reach with your proposed marketing?

The Competition

Regardless of whether your product or service is new or already on the market, who or what are your competitors? Are they direct competition? Are they well established and able to withstand your efforts? Where are the competitors' marketing areas? If direct competition exists, how does your offering stack up in terms of quality, price, or benefits? If it's a new product, is it easy to duplicate? Will you be able to protect it?

PLAN FOR THE BEST AND PROTECT YOURSELF AGAINST THE WORST

How often do we hear stories about people and companies having to close or enter bankruptcy? And why is it that we keep hearing nine out of ten new businesses will fail or close within two years?

Any number of reasons that can explain why businesses fail:

- Low sales volume
- Insufficient capital
- Wrong location
- Incorrect merchandise
- Competition that is too strong
- Ineffective advertising
- Changing market conditions
- Poor management
- Lack of know how

If you want to go into business and want the best chance of making a go of it, there is something you can do: Prepare for the best and protect yourself against the worst.

You can plan ahead. It's no mystery. Successful business owners are those who don't try to reinvent the wheel, have wisely taken good counsel, done it right, and come out on top.

One thing is for sure: Anybody who runs any business bigger than a lemonade stand will find out quickly that the most efficient way to get seed money or financing for your business is to write a plan. Banks, venture capitalists, private investors, even smart friends, and relatives insist on it. Even if you could get all the start-up money you need, without having a plan, you're only fooling yourself. The woods are full of people who went into business with just a good idea and an expectation of steady sales, only to end up in bankruptcy court. The court will insist you work up a plan, only then it will be called a reorganization plan.

Whether you write out a few pages of notes or prepare a well-thought-out and carefully detailed document, you will need to know where you are, where you're going and where you can expect to be. Here's the payoff: the most important reason to plan ahead is that you'll discover how you can manage your business more profitably. The truth is, planning will not ensure your success. But nothing will give you a greater chance of success than preparing a carefully crafted plan and following it.

CHARACTERISTICS OF A SUCCESSFUL SMALL BUSINESS OPERATOR

This great country is indeed the "land of opportunity." Nowhere else in the world can you control your destiny as completely as you can if you're fortunate

5

enough to be living in the United States. Every time we sing "the Star Spangled Banner" we are reminded that our country is the "land of the free and the home of the brave." In most cases, however, too few are brave enough to venture out on the road to freedom. For those of us who have made this venture, however, few would choose to go back.

Success in small business is not a matter left to chance or change. You have heard of successful entrepreneurs who were lucky or in the right place at the right time. Luck or good timing is not something you can count on, nor will it carry you through years of operating a business successfully. Furthermore, successful small business operators, really make their own luck, and put themselves in the right place at the right time.

American small business operators number in the millions. Of the approximately 25 million businesses in this country, more than 95% or over 23 million are operated as sole proprietorships; in other words, most small businesses in America are run by people who are in business for themselves.

Who are these people we call successful small business operators? While there are no absolutes, we can make some general observations about them:

1. They *love to make money*. Some enjoy the things that money can buy; others view money as just a way of measuring success; still others see money as power, financial security, or means of positive self-esteem.
2. They have *bigger dreams* than most other people. They challenge themselves to do more because they want more - more of the money, freedom and status that accompany small business ownership.
3. Successful small business owners are intensely *success oriented*. They have a need - sometimes a burning desire - to succeed. They need to prove themselves, to their friends and acquaintances, to their families, and to their toughest critics - themselves.

6

4. Small business owners **work harder** than most people. Some even think working 18 hours a day is fun. They don't mind putting in extra effort with the prospect of reaping the rewards. Successful people do not like to work hard so someone else can reap the rewards. Maybe that's why, as a group, they don't like working for other people.

5. Small Business Owners are **better at something** than most people. Some have outstanding artistic talent; others are brilliant marketers; still others have a natural gift for organizing; and most are born leaders. They have something extra that will help them succeed, and they are smart enough to make the most of it.

6. Successful small business operators **look at risks differently** than most people do. They understand the basic risk and reward ratio of life: the greater the risks, the greater the rewards. In other words, no guts, no glory. They accept the fact that they can't win if they're not in the game. But their risks are almost always carefully calculated and supported by confidence and belief in themselves. They reduce the risk by learning the odds and knowing what they're doing.

7. Small business owners are **proud of their abilities** and their achievements. Their success proves that they are not average or mediocre. Success gives them great satisfaction -- and pride!

ARE YOU READY?

Even before you think about what goes into your planning, think about your needs and desires. Operating a business is a lot different than checking into work in the morning, doing a job and collecting a paycheck at the end of the week. Make no mistake, operating a business is hard work, with long hours and lots of complications: from quality control, to hiring and managing people, to keeping up a constant cash flow. And if you're the right kind of person, you'll thrive on it.

Many years of research and studies of successful entrepreneurs found that business ownership attracts certain kinds of people. If you fit the profile, you probably have the right stuff to go out on your own. If you don't, you will want to think about developing some of these traits:

7

- Initiative, the first and most important quality
- Independence and a healthy ego
- Desire to maintain firm control over your future
- Organizational ability to get others to work with you
- Drive and enthusiasm
- Emotional stability for tough times and for success
- Self-confidence, with high standards for yourself and others
- Willingness to learn new things and sacrifice for success
- Willingness to take calculated risks
- Good communication abilities
- A sense of humor

Without these characteristics, it's back to the drawing board. Obviously any of these personality traits is a mix of positive and negative qualities. The same kind of hard driving personality that generates the creative energy to start a business can also destroy it. The trick is to know yourself and know how to channel the best of what you've got.

If you reflect most of the good qualities in the preceding list you are the kind of person who will have the best chance to build a business and reap its rewards. You will also know some of the reasons why otherwise capable businesspeople fail. What makes some businesses successful will be one of the most important things you'll learn in this book.

GET STARTED!

There are only two things you can be sure of about going into business: One is that you will be going into partnership with the government - it may have a lot to say about how you conduct your business and will certainly have a hand in your profits; the other thing you can count on is change.

You already have much of the information you need. You've probably been thinking about going into business or developing your business for months or years. You have been gathering fragments of information and planning what you'll do when you get going. The idea looks good or you wouldn't have gotten as far as reading this book. The time has come to get it out of your mind or off the scraps of paper you've collected and put it together into a blueprint that leads you to action.

Here's one important hint about what it really takes to make it in business: The quality of management and the quality of marketing are the two most essential factors, and they begin with knowing yourself and your business. What about financing? Though it's important, management and marketing will go a long way to determining how you get the capital you need.

In the next section you will learn about the first step in planning; what kind of business is best for you and whether you should start up fresh, buy an existing business or look into franchising.

CHAPTER 2

Single Biggest Mistake Small Business Make...And How To Avoid It

---

"There is only one valid definition of business purpose: to create a customer."

--Peter Drucker (1909-2005) Austrian-born management consultant and writer

---

There is one secret reason, one secret formula that can make your small business a true success, faster and bigger than your current dreams. But rarely does anyone talk about this one factor that separates successful small businesses from the struggling others. It is not taught in undergraduate or master's entrepreneurship programs. The Small Business Administration doesn't mention it. Big business isn't using it except in rare cases. Bankers don't understand it. It is the most valuable asset a business can own, even though it is not on any financial statement.

Owners that know and understand the power of this one secret can generate money whenever they need or want it, can get clients to spend more and more with them on command, and can provide customer service way beyond their customer's expectations.

This one asset is something that allows the business to keep running even though the business may have burned down, been ruined by hurricane or many other unforeseen events.

It is SO IMPORTANT that it is covered in detail in its own chapter. But what is it that creates a successful business?

The secret to small business success is… YOUR CLIENT LIST. Before you turn up your nose and quit reading, finish this chapter to understand the real power your client list holds for you. After reading, you can choose to follow your own path. But it will be the longer, more painful path to take.

Example #1

Martha opened up a store in October of this year. The store had makeup, hair accessories and bath products targeted at "tweener" (young people between 6-13 years old) girls. Martha was doing really well when she first opened, even though the store

was only open on Fridays, Saturdays and Sundays. Each weekend, Martha had at least 30-50 girls purchasing products from her store. In April, sales started to slow down. Martha needed to raise some cash quickly to pay her rent.

Martha was running out of cash quickly. After trying everything she could think of, Martha called Susan Johnson, a business consultant she had met at a conference. Susan figured out Martha had seen

11

over 1,100 girls in her store since October.

"One of the fastest ways you can generate cash is to send a postcard to all the girls who had been to the store," suggested Susan. "These girls have been to the store and are familiar with all the great stuff there, they don't get a lot of mail, and if you offer them something special like: "Buy One lip gloss, Get One FREE", there will surely be many that come back into the store." After Susan had finished with her idea, she waited for a response from Martha.

After quite a while without an answer, Susan asked Martha if she liked the idea.

Martha quietly said, "I don't have any of the names."

The harsh reality is, without any customer names built over time, it is very difficult to generate sales whenever you want or need. It is very difficult and expensive to get new customers into your business without any prior relationship. If you start keeping your client list and continue to communicate with them, you will be more successful than you can possibly imagine.

Your most valuable asset in your business is **YOUR CLIENT LIST**. You could have the best employees, the best product, even one that cures cancer, but if you don't have customers, you don't have a business.

IMPORTANCE OF YOUR CLIENT LIST

Why is it important to keep your client list? As you saw above, it can keep you in business in slow times, and without a client list it can rapidly put you out of business. Having a client list gives you power and freedom that struggling business owners don't have and don't understand.

It is important to keep your client list for the following reasons:

1) Cheaper marketing
2) Current customers are more likely to spend again with you
3) You could be even more successful
4) Generate cash when you need it
5) Disservice to your customers if you don't keep it
6) Creates you in the toll-position

Cheaper Marketing

Many studies have been done on marketing to a "cold" (no relationship) and "warm" (established relationship). The "warm" list always outperforms the "cold" list. What does that mean to you?

If you examine a typical direct mail campaign, you will notice that a normal response is less than 1%. So for every 100 you mail, you will get about 1 interested person. But if you mail 100 postcards to your customer list, the response can be anywhere from 5%-50% depending on the offer. If it costs you the same amount to send the 100 postcards no matter who you send them to, then you will make more on your client list compared to the "cold" list. See below:

Your product is $10
You mail 100 postcards at 25 cents each = $25

Cold list return 1% or 1 which results in 1 sale = $10
Your customers list returns 25% which results in 25 sales = $250

The cold list will actually lose money for you:

$10 (for 1 sale) - $25 (postcard cost) = **- $15 Loss**

But mailing to your list generates a profit:

$250 (25 sales at $10 each) - $25 (postcard cost) = **$225 Profit**

As you can see, marketing to your own customer list can be the difference between

13

success and failure to your business. It is much cheaper to market to your customer list than it is to a list of names that do not have a relationship with you and your business.

Clients are more likely to spend with you again

Why would your clients spend with you instead of someone else? When someone does business with you and becomes a customer, they have started to form a relationship with you. As long as you continue to meet their expectations, they will continue to do business with you.

Consumers like to know what to expect when they do business with someone. It is actually "risky" to do business with a new company. Since you have taken away the risk, your customers are more likely to continue to buy from you instead of someone else.

As you learned from the previous example, previous customers will more likely do business with you again and again and again if you give them a chance and a specific reason to come back.

You Could Be Even More Successful

If there was one secret you could learn from this book, it would be, the secret to building a business faster and more profitable than you have dreamed, you need a client list. Every business owner who does not keep this information is "leaving money on the table" every day.

Maybe your business is so successful; you don't think you need to keep your customer's information. But, what you don't realize is that if you continued to market to your customers, you would be making even more money than you are right now. You are actually losing money by not marketing to your list every month.

If you are in a business where you do not have capacity to service any new customers, then you need to increase your prices. You will actually make some room for higher paying customers than the ones you are currently servicing.

Generate Money When You Need It Or Want It

Having a client list gives you control over the business, instead of the business having control over you. It allows you to generate cash whenever you need it or want it.

With a client list, you can send them an offer whenever you want to generate extra cash. Maybe you would like to take a vacation with your family. Send a postcard or email with a special offer for your products or services if you customers act within a certain timeframe. If the offer is good enough, some customers will come forward and will purchase. A large enough customer list and an irresistible offer, will generate income almost every time.

Marketing to your list and not having to rely on bringing in new customers every day gives you the freedom to run the business instead of the business running you.

Disservice To Your Customers

In reality, when you don't market to your customers on a continual basis, you are really doing them and yourself a disservice. Although this may sound confusing, here is a quick story to explain.

There is a yarn shop down the street from Karen's office. Karen is a rookie knitter who  only knows one stitch and has made only a couple of scarves. Karen has been into the store a couple of times, but they never ask her for her name, address or email. At this point, Karen couldn't go to a big craft store to buy yarn because once she finishes a project; she doesn't know how to get it off the needles.

Karen enjoys knitting, but doesn't even know what type of project people make after a scarf. All the projects that Karen knows about seem too complicated. So Karen is

15

relying on the small yarn shop to help her. But Karen doesn't really know what questions to ask, so she doesn't ask any.

Little does the yarn shop know that if they send Karen a postcard or email about upcoming classes, new types of yarn, or other projects that one could do, Karen would be back to buy more yarn. But since the yarn store doesn't ask Karen for her contact information, they have no way to contact or find Karen again.

So Karen goes on to a different type of hobby and the yarn shop loses a valuable customer and sales. Karen would have continued to purchase expensive yarns, if the yarn shop would have helped her to enjoy the hobby more.

As you can see, NOT marketing to your customers is doing you and your customers a disservice because regardless of what business you are in, your customer do not know how you can help them further if you don't tell them. You lose sales, they lose the enjoyment of working with you or purchasing products that could make their lives better.

Once a customer has had an enjoyable experience with you, they trust you and would like to do more work with you. But you can't give them that chance if you don't continue to stay in contact with them through your marketing.

Key To Success

Your customer list is your Key To Success. Asking for and keeping your customer's information is the first step to being able to market to them long term. It isn't about the product they purchased today, it is about building a relationship where they will continue to purchase many more products in the future.

Your client list is really your Key To Success in any business.

16

HOW TO CREATE A CLIENT LIST

But where do you start with a customer list?

If you are still "thinking" about starting a business, you can start creating your client list. Everyone should start by writing down everyone you know personally. Make a list of the following people and as much information as you know about them.

- Family
  - Father, mother, in-laws
  - Everyone else – family tree
- Friends
  - Current
  - Past
  - College friends
- Mentors
- People you have done business with
  - Barber
  - Grocer
  - Pharmacy
- Teachers – your own and your children's
- Neighbors – old and current
- Business associates
- People you worked for
- People who worked for you
- People you worked with - colleagues
- Customers for your company
- Vendors for your company
- Consultants for your company
- Contractors for your company

17

- Professionals that work with your company

- People you worked with in the past

- Person who hired you

- Person who you hired

- Do this for current jobs and past jobs

You may think that you can do it on your own. You may be able to, but why make it harder on yourself than you have to? The majority of people on your personal list will want to know what you are doing and will want to support you. Don't limit your success by keeping your friends, family and acquaintances off your list. You never know who they know that could be your first million dollar client or that hard-to-find supplier.

After you have created a list of people you know, you will want to start adding customers who are doing business with you. If you don't have any customers yet, start creating a list of places you could connect with to build your list. Will you focus your clients on a geographic basis or a demographic (characteristics like income level, gender age etc)? How will you easily bring clients to you?

HOW TO MANAGE ALL THE CLIENT INFORMATION

The first thing you will need is a system to keeping all the client information. This system should be easy to access with the data in a useable format. Basic systems can be started with 3 X 5 index cards or 3-ring or spiral notebooks. The biggest disadvantage with these systems is that it is difficult to print mailing addresses or emails in an electronic format. If you were doing a mailing, you would have to manually write all the names and addresses. If these systems work for you, then start

18

using them. It is more important to start capturing your client's information than what format you keep the data.

If you want to try something more electronic, you could use anything from Microsoft Excel ™, ACT! or an online application like www.Salesforce.com. For a trial version of www.salesforce.com for small business visit our website at www.aisb.biz/resources.html. ACT! and www.salesforce.com are also Customer Relationship Management (CRM) solutions. CRM is effective for companies that want or need to keep track of discussions with clients over a period of time. With both of these solutions, you can keep track of letters they received and conversations made with the clients. Many of these programs allow you to perform a mail-merge into a letter or to print labels, so you don't have to write the addresses manually.

If you have staff working for you, make sure they understand the importance of gathering client information. Typically the owner understands the importance of gathering the data, but the receptionist at the front desk or sales clerks in your store do not fully understand and therefore do not follow through. Each client you miss will cost you later through lost sales.

The best way to add customers to your list is to make it a weekly goal. Create an incentive program for the staff person who adds the largest number of new client names and/or birthdays in a week.

WHAT INFORMATION SHOULD YOU GATHER

Whenever you are working with customers, you have to determine how much information to gather. The more the better for you, but not always for the customer. Although you may want to collect a lot of information, you may find your customers

19

resistant to giving too much information.

The main reason you want to collect as much as possible is that marketing laws and rules change over time. Here are some examples:

- If you were only collecting consumer names and phone numbers, you lost your marketing in March 2003 when the do-not-call list came in to effect.

- In the business to business market, you could no longer fax without permission as of July 2005.

- Currently there is legislation about sending emails. The Can-Spam Act, effective January 2004 specifically addresses who can send commercial emails. If were collecting only name and email, your marketing would be dramatically affected.

As a basic rule, you should try to gather (but it will be based on your customer's thoughts also):

1) Name
2) Address (street address, city, state, zip, country (on the internet))
3) Email
4) Phone
5) Fax (For Business Clients)
6) Birthday (if you plan to use Birthday marketing)

Any information is better than nothing. Your collection of data should be what you feel comfortable with and how you plan to use the data. What types of marketing will be most effective for you?

WHAT IF CLIENT'S DON'T WANT TO GIVE THEIR INFORMATION?

Many consumers are tired of giving up their information to everyone. It seems that most of the large retail companies have been gathering information from clients and "over-using" the data.

If you find your customers are reluctant to give you their data, you can try a couple of different things.

- First, communicate your plans with them. Explain to them how you plan to communicate with them and how often. Unless you have a very targeted list of over 10,000 names, you probably wouldn't want to be selling or sharing the names with any other company. If you are sending a postcard quarterly or one about an annual sale, you will get more people to sign up. If you are doing a daily email, you will get less people to sign up.

- Second, give them an incentive. In the internet world, there is almost always an incentive. It may be a free, valuable e-newsletter (ezine) or a free report or another bonus gift. In a brick and mortar store, you can also use incentives. One store may use an annual 20%-50% off coupon. It may be advance notice of a huge sale. It may be priority access to an attorney, accountant or consultant. Customers always like something for free and therefore it is a good way to build up your customer list.

Always remember: your customer list is YOUR MOST VALUABLE ASSET. Even though bankers and educators don't fully understand the power of this secret, doesn't mean you shouldn't be using it. Having a customer list of people who know you and trust you can accelerate your success. It is much cheaper and more effective to market to this list. The clients will spend more with you over time and will be there whenever you need or want more cash. In reality, not keeping your customer's data and continuing to communicate with them, is doing not only your business a disservice in lost sales, but is a disservice to your customers. They don't know the questions that they need to be asking, so help them.

Finally, keeping the information and what to ask for may be challenges along the way. But try to give your customer comfort by communicating with them how you plan to use the information and perhaps giving them an incentive to help you build your business.

CHAPTER 3

Starting up, Buying or Franchising

Think about this: an average of 500,000 new businesses have been started in the United States every year over the past ten years. That's a lot of competition. But every year many thousands of men and women start the same way, and succeed, with just an idea and a little money they've begged, borrowed or dug out of their savings.

Being in charge of your own business does not necessarily mean starting from scratch. It does not mean having to do it the hard or slow way. If you have some money to begin with or can convince a few friends or relatives to pitch in, it may be to your advantage to buy an existing business. It's like finding your dream house: You can build it from scratch, or you can wait until you come across the right one and buy it. In the first case, it's a little harder on your nerves. In the second case, harder on your pocketbook. Take your pick. A third option is franchising, which may minimize your risk, since you're offering a proven product and have the support of franchiser services.

STARTING UP

Figure 2.1 summarizes the advantages and disadvantages of the start-up option for small business. Take the case of Jeffrey Anderson, who had put in 15 years at a large management consultation firm in upstate New York. He generally liked his job, but had become dissatisfied.

Figure 2.1 Start-up business

Advantages:	*Disadvantages:*
■ Fulfills the desire for complete business independence	■ You must provide all the capital
■ Freedom to establish your preferred location	■ Potential competitors may present problems
■ Choice of suppliers, sources and employees	■ Harder to estimate how much it will cost to get into business
■ Create your own customer target profile	■ No past history of return on your investment
■ Redecoration or enlargement to fit your own needs	■ Maximum of risk and investment
■ New equipment, fixtures and leases	■ On your own in site location, training, financing, marketing, promotion, and record keeping
■ Fresh supplies, inventory and materials	■ Most new ventures require a few years of intensive effort before profits start rolling in
■ No royalties to pay to a franchiser No franchisor or seller to tell you how you run your business.	

It was the same grind every day, and he was getting bored. From time to time he considered going into business for himself, but never really got active until he came up with a business idea that appealed to his considerable interest in music. The idea was to open a record store, but one with a difference, offering a 20 percent discount for customers who would join his club and agree to buy at least ten records a year.

Anderson did some research into the retail record business and decided that, despite the heavy local competition, he had a good chance of success with his discount idea. Anderson rented a 2,000-square-foot storefront in the downtown business section and secured a $45,000 loan through the Small Business Administration.

From the beginning he was faced with two problems: competing in a crowded market and bringing in enough money to make up for the discounts he gave on his records. There were a few years when he had to hang on by his fingernails. But with a basically good idea and persistence, Anderson was able to make a go of it in a business he really enjoyed, despite his long working hours. Today, thanks to a unique idea and careful attention to customer wants, an enlarged Anderson's Music Shop sells more recordings than any of his competitors in the marketing area.

Unquestionably there are opportunities for new businesses to succeed in the marketplace. Anderson found a position in the business world and made good by providing customers with a product and service they wanted. This attention to the customer is at the core of most successful businesses.

Product, service and profit are three vital ingredients for running a successful business, but they can also be used to decide what business to get into. Prospective business owners too often choose a business simply because it seems like fun or easy, without thinking about whether the business will meet customer demand. At the same time, attention must be given to the need for profitable sales volume. Without customer demand, there are too few sales, and without sales, no

25

business can succeed.

Top New Businesses

Business ideas are created from countless sources: hobbies, market gaps, and technological advances and others. According to government statistics, some of the most popular and successful new business areas include:

- Accounting services
- Auto parts
- Automobile/truck rental service
- Car washes
- Carpet cleaning
- Convenience stores
- Copying establishments
- Diet services
- Draperies
- Employment placement services
- Fast food
- Car care centers
- Hair care
- Laundry and dry cleaning services

- Lawn care
- Leisure and travel
- Muffler replacement
- Picture frames
- Pre-school and school age educational services
- Printing
- Real estate outlets
- Retail tire outlets
- Sewer and drain cleaning
- Tax preparation
- Transmission shops

From Entrepreneur Magazine's 6th Annual Million Dollar Ideas from January 2007, here are the businesses they believe are the next HOT businesses:

Food Businesses
- Tea
- Online Specialty Foods
- Do-It-Yourself Meal Preparation
- One-Product Restaurants
- Chocolate Cafes

Security Services
- Shredding
- ID-Theft Prevention and Recovery
- Hosted Security Provider
- Data Backup

Tech Products
- Mobile Add-Ons
- Aftermarket Accessories

Home Improvement Services
- Home Staging
- Senior Retrofitting

B2B Services
- Technology Consulting
- Staffing

- Tech Recycling

Kid Businesses
- Kids' Party/Activity Centers
- Child Care
- Teaching Toys
- Education & Tutoring Products & Services
- Cooking for Kids
- Kids' Hair Salons

- E-Tail for Kids
- Tween Tech

Miscellaneous Businesses
- Travel with a Purpose
- eBay Aftermarket
- Patient Advocacy
- Niche Exercise Accessories

And these are just a few of the kinds of businesses that people are starting every day. When you decide to start a business, make sure it's right for you. Be careful to find out if you really have the skills necessary to run the venture you've chosen. The more background you have in a particular business, the more likely you are to succeed. While some people have an inherent ability to succeed in whatever business they try, most of us find it wiser to stick to something we know. Starting or running your own business is a difficult, time-consuming undertaking. You lessen the risk of failure if you bring some experience into the mix.

The following are some of the questions you must ask yourself in the earliest stages of your business development:

- Is your product or service new or established?
- Do you have skills or experience that relate?
- What size of business can you handle?
- Do you intend to go it alone? With employees?
- Is there a preferred or ideal location?
- How much of your own capital is available?
- How much additional capital can you raise?
- Are partners being considered? For capital? For helpful skills?
- Are you going to run the business on a part-time or full-time basis?

Every business and businessperson has limitations and every business has just so much financing available. It's best to know at the outset what you can handle and how many problems you can juggle at one time.

Can You Handle the Investment?

The desire to go into business is one thing; the most important financial consideration is the minimum amount of capital required. This is what it will cost you to get the business started and keep it running for at least one year. For the small businessperson, the less expensive an operation is, the more realistic a prospect it becomes.

In the next chapter, we will discuss the Five Money Keys for business success. Money Key #5 states: The successful small businessperson knows how to find and use someone else's money in order to make money! This is particularly true if you're starting up a business that requires a large initial investment. For example, assume you will need $100,000 over and above what you have available in your own cash or liquid assets to get the business going. Where and how are you going to raise this money? Will you be able to borrow from a friend? Are you going to take in a partner? Will you seek out a bank loan or a Small Business Administration guaranteed loan, or will you seek out a private investor?

Regardless of where you will turn for outside financing, it is clear that Money Key #5 will be most important in order for you to start your business.

If you are going to buy an existing business for about $100,000, you'll still have to find the start-up money from lenders, but you'll have an additional help. Many business owners are willing to accept as little as 20 percent down on the purchase and then allow you to pay them the rest on a monthly basis, out of profits.

BUYING A BUSINESS

Once you've decided what kind of a business you want to be in, the first question to ask is whether you start your own or buy an existing one. Many experts

Figure 2.2 Buying a Business

Advantages:	Disadvantages:
▪ Location is established	▪ The lease may be expiring
▪ Relationships with suppliers, sources all set up	▪ Redecoration or enlargement may be required
▪ Experienced employees are available	▪ Location may be poor
▪ Business records ready to help you plan	▪ Equipment may be outdated.
▪ Previous owner's experience is available while you are learning the business	▪ Inventory may be mediocre or old
▪ You know exactly how much it will cost to get into the business	▪ Current Employee problems
▪ Past profit picture and return on your investment can be more easily predicted	▪ Previous owner may have had unethical business practices that will affect the new business
▪ A favorable purchase price may be negotiated	▪ Potential competitors may present problems
▪ Shortens time it takes to establish the new business	▪ Poor financial records
▪ Customers are available immediately	▪ An unwise purchase due to desire to get started
▪ Initial financial outlay may be	▪ Overall purchase price can be

less than a new start-up • Equipment, fixtures and leases are all set up • Supplies, inventory or materials are ready to go	high • Relationships with customers and suppliers may be unsatisfactory

and owners believe that it's best to buy an existing business. The reasons are simple to see and there are many advantages and some disadvantages, as summarized in Figure 2.2.

With all these benefits, it's easy to understand why buying an established business is so often considered the best way to go. For first-time business owner with little or no experience, it can often seem to be a much safer way to ease into the business world. Equally important is the fact that the business buyer is established immediately. Most new, start-from-scratch ventures require a few years of intensive effort before profits start rolling in.

All the advantages of buying an existing business assume one thing: that the business you're buying is free of or has limited flaws. Just as when you buy a used car, it pays to be cautious. In almost every case, there will be problems to be overcome. One problem that frequently crops up is that the business seller doesn't want to accept a reasonable price because he or she confuses the value of the business (return on investment) with income (return on investment plus salary).

As with any purchase, the disadvantages of buying a business must be carefully thought about and considered, even if the deal goes through, as a means of getting the best purchase price.

Where To Find Businesses For Sale

The classified ads and business sections of local newspapers and The Wall Street Journal are full of business opportunities ads, offering businesses for sale.

Likewise, you can advertise in these sections your interest in purchasing a business. You can place a classified ad in your local newspaper, usually under the listing title of "business opportunity wanted," or you can place a display ad in the business section of the paper. If you do not want to advertise your name or wish to keep people from knowing who you are, the newspaper will provide you with a return box number to which people can respond.

You may also get help from your lawyer or banker, who often will hear about people who for one reason or another want to sell their businesses. You may also want to send a letter to accountants, who often have clients that want to sell their businesses. Still other sources include business brokers, real estate agents and companies, business finders and firms, business opportunity shows and franchise shows.

If you really want to be bold and imaginative, then consider this: If you see a business that you like and would like to consider purchasing it, simply stop by or call the owner for an appointment. On meeting with the owner, state that you may be interested in purchasing his or her business. There is an old saying, "He or she who asks, gets."

Still another source for locating a business that may be for sale is to talk with the managers of the shopping centers of your area. They often are the first to hear when one of their tenants wishes to retire or sell their business.

A wide number of magazines that advertise different business opportunities for sale: Money, Entrepreneur, Income Opportunities, Success, and Business Start-Ups just to mention a few. These and many more can be found in your local library or at a nearby newsstand.

If anyone is looking for a business, you can not forget the Internet. The largest sites listing businesses for sale are:

www.bizbuysell.com
www.businessesforsale.com
www.sunbeltnetwork.com

Buying the Company vs. Buying the Assets

Imagine the following plot: You have your eyes on Smith & Smith, Inc. It is a small, family-run business that manufactures rubber seals and gaskets. For the most part, the company consists of a workshop, including several machines, raw materials, an inventory of completed gaskets waiting for customers, some office furniture and equipment, and a delivery truck. Your initial negotiations indicate that Helen and Howard Smith are willing to sell for about $250,000.

The issue to be decided is whether you should purchase the corporation itself or only its assets. In the first case, you would purchase all the stock, the shares that are held by the Smiths; in the second case, you would buy only the material assets used by the company in its business.

As a general rule, you are better off buying just the assets because "you get what you see". This allows you to limit your liabilities or unknowns that you have received from the previous owner. From a financial point of view, you can claim immediate tax deductions for the inventory and other depreciable property.

Get a Lawyer

If you do find an existing business that seems like a good deal to take over, try to reach a verbal agreement with the owner on the major terms. Then see your lawyer right away. Besides offering legal protection, your lawyer will most likely help you in contract negotiations by obtaining useful supplementary information and data. He or she will give you valuable feedback before you leap into the water, before you put your signature on what might be the biggest deal of your life.

In addition to drafting the contract, your lawyer can review and evaluate documents prepared by the seller's lawyer and ask crucial questions that you might not have thought of asking. Your lawyer can represent you at the closing procedures to ensure that all documents are handled correctly and to your advantage.

Your lawyer can also make you aware of what you need to know about the business. He or she can help you identify documents and records including existing leases for equipment, contracts for deed, pending lawsuits, federal requirements, and much more. Most important, an attorney can make sure that you don't sign before the other party has put all cards on the table.

Another important advantage an attorney can give you is positive or critical comments about the chances of the new business. When you don't have family members with relevant business experience, your attorney is the one who can listen patiently and can give objective advice when you spill out your hopes, fears and dreams for the future. Running a business can mean making good money; at the same time, it also means taking a risk. You need someone you can rely on; someone who will warn you before a potential risk turns into an actual disaster.

The Contract

Any contracts you make should be as detailed as possible. Don't be afraid of being a stickler. Have the seller list and briefly describe each item: equipment or parts thereof; vehicles; fixtures; furniture; inventory and raw materials, by number, weight or volume; work in progress; existing leases; rental agreements; patents; and real estate.

Make sure you have a written statement indicating who will be liable for the debts of the company at the time of the transaction. If it's you, make sure you

33

know absolutely their full extent. In addition, there should be an agreement stating who is entitled to the accounts receivable. Be prudent and realistic. You may have trouble collecting some or all of the money outstanding, especially as a retailer in poorer neighborhoods.

After you have taken the preceding into consideration and have negotiated the purchase price, ask for an itemized statement, mainly for tax purposes. Here is an example:

Merchandise on hand	$ 80,000
Tangible personal property	$150,000
Lease agreements	$ 10,000
Good will/trade name	$ 10,000
Total purchase price	$ 250,000

If you have not already done so, this is the time to check with your financial source to determine how his or her people would feel about the deal and exactly how much they will be willing to provide to make it all work out.

Purchase Price Adjustments   The idea of adjustments to the purchase price becomes especially important if there is a considerable time lag between the drawing of the contract and closing. So in setting out the purchase price, allow for adjustments. For example, make provisions for how to handle increases or decreases in merchandise on hand (inventory). One option might be to stipulate that you will pay up to $50,000 for inventory at closing, based on seller's invoice cost. If the actual inventory at closing exceeds this amount, you reserve the option of purchasing the difference, possibly at a discount.

Other adjustment provisions could include such items as pre-payments for rent or leases, utilities or insurance premiums, license fees and property taxes. Another important factor is salaries and wages.   If they are paid at the end of

34

each month retroactively and you take over the business at any other time, the purchase price should be reduced to allow for the fact that you are going to pay salaries for periods when the seller still owned the business.

Your purchase contract also should indicate when the payment for the company is due and how it will be executed (by check or promissory note, for example). Try to negotiate and be as creative as you can in your proposals. There are almost no restrictions or limits on the type of terms you can have if the seller consents.

Some transfers involve seller financing. Obviously, the number of installments and the applicable interest rate are key items for negotiations. In some instances, installments are tied to the profit generated during the first five years under new ownership. In those situations, the seller was willing or forced to continue to share in the risk of the business.

Most deals require a deposit when the contract is signed. Pay special attention at this point. Keep the deposit as small as you can and have in writing that it actually applies against the purchase price. Don't allow it to be treated as a form of fee. If you stretch your payments over an extended period of time, it's not unreasonable for the seller to retain a security interest in some of the major assets until payment has been made in full. Corresponding arrangements should be part of the general contract. In such a case, expect limited ownership or usage of major property items.

Think about these potential problems:

- The lease may be expiring and negotiations are needed.
- Redecoration or enlargement may be required.
- Location may be in a declining area.
- Equipment may require replacement or repair.

35

- Inventory may be unbalanced and/or outdated.

- Employees may be unionized, complicating contract terms.

- Relationships with customers and suppliers may have deteriorated.

- Profit potential may be endangered by stronger present or potential competitors.

- Financial records may not be a true reflection of value. This is a job for an accountant.

- Your desire to get started may cause an unwise purchase.

- Overall purchase price can be higher than the initial costs of a new start-up.

WHAT ABOUT FRANCHISING?

Figure 2.3 summarizes advantages and disadvantages of the small business option for franchising. The appeal of franchising for the independent businessperson is that it is a practical and economic means of fulfilling his or her desire for independence with a minimum of risk and investment and maximum opportunities for success through the use of a proven product or service and a proven marketing method. Franchising is a way to be in business for yourself, but not by yourself.

The franchisee is an independent business owner who pays the franchiser for the right to put this recipe for success to use. As a franchisee you provide all or nearly all the working capital to establish and develop the outlet. There is a continuous financial relationship, usually including a fee paid in advance, plus a continuing royalty based on an established percentage of gross revenues.

Some franchisors will supply financial assistance to the franchisee to pay the initial and ongoing costs of conducting the business. Although an attractive extra, financial assistance should not be considered as a major decision factor or a substitute for very careful, thorough investigation into all the facts in your choice of any franchise. It is simply another element that can be put into the mix.

Ideally, when you purchase a franchise, you are also purchasing a pre-packaged business. Although you own every part of it, you have a partner, your franchisor, who can insist or sometimes merely suggest how you run your business.

Why Do People Buy Franchises?

For the new entrepreneur, a franchise often makes it easier to go into business, because it cuts down on the amount of capital required and provides a sense of security through the experience and help offered by the franchisor. Franchising is one good way for some small business operators to avoid problems that can ruin a business.

The franchisor will usually help in such areas as site location, management training, financing, marketing, promotion, and record keeping. The franchisee, in return, agrees to operate under the conditions specified by the franchiser.

Figure 2.3 Buying a Franchise

Advantages:	*Disadvantages:*
▪ Be in business for yourself, not by yourself	▪ Pay the franchiser for the right to use its program
▪ Help in such areas as site location, training, financing, marketing, promotion, and record keeping	▪ Provide all or nearly all the working capital to establish and develop the business
▪ Proven marketing methods	▪ A continuous financial relationship
▪ Minimum of risk and investment	▪ Fee paid in advance
▪ A way to avoid problems that can ruin a business.	▪ A continuing royalty based on a percentage of gross revenues.

• Security from experience and help the franchiser provides • Often reduces the amount of capital required • A pre-packaged business you own • Proven product or service • Maximum opportunities for success	• The franchiser, can insist or suggest how you run your business. • Franchisee must agree to operate under specific conditions

THE BUSINESS CLIMATE

Whether yours is a start up, an established businesses or a franchise, it is always important to be aware of financial matters that can affect the profitability of your business.

Four key factors that can affect the performance of businesses are:

- Trends in the national economy
- Trends in your regional and local economies
- Trends in the industry or service in which you are involved
- The impact of new or proposed governmental (Federal, state and local) legislation and regulations on your business.

Although national economic indicators will show general trends, it's important to watch indicators that affect the local economic situation.

Understanding indicators such as local unemployment and inflation figures and interest rates will help you make financing and general business decisions. For example, higher interest rates could mean borrowing will be more expensive for small business, and lower interest rates may mean that you can borrow funds at lower cost. If unemployment figures are high and recession is likely, the local economy may not be receptive to the promotion of a new product

38

or service or an additional location of an established business. Information about local indicators and forecasts can be found in local newspapers.

In addition to area indicators, it's important to understand local economic trends or developments. An expansion of services or introduction of a new product line by a large local employer could be a sign of the company's optimism toward future consumer spending. When major area employers are reducing their labor forces or when businesses seem to be closing their doors, the signal may be that the economy is slowing or stagnating.

Stay abreast of trends within your industry as well. For example, watch for new products that could be included in the present product line or any technological developments that may lower costs of production. Remember that trends and developments can benefit the competition as well, so keep in step by watching trends and technology carefully. Trade associations and industry newsletters can provide such information.

Federal and state legislation can influence your decision-making, directly and indirectly. For example, minimum wage legislation, importing or exporting regulations, or legislation that may prohibit the use of certain materials or chemicals are examples of federal legislation. Instances where state legislation affects small business are changes in sales tax or workers compensation, for example. The impact of legislation is often not felt immediately. This gives you time to adjust to new developments or regulations.

Pay close attention to economic indicators and information and use these tools in selecting and running your business. By tracking this type of information, your business expectations will be more realistic and planning objectives will be more practical.

CHAPTER 4

Success and The

Five Money Keys

This chapter is about the role money plays in having a successful business. It describes the Five Money Keys that have helped so many people like you reach business success. It will point out the importance of knowing the product or service you are selling, and that important ingredient, sales expertise, that makes it all work together.

We're going to talk about competition and the skills you already have or should develop before you even seek financing, because knowing yourself is the vital ingredient to getting others to give you money and making a go of whatever business you want to build and prosper.

In this chapter you will learn:

- The five Money Keys that will make your business a success.
- How you can learn valuable lessons from your competition.
- The capabilities it will take to make you successful a business operator.

No matter what skills or talents you bring to the business world, it is extremely unlikely that you will be a winner in this highly competitive world if you are not serious about money. Business is not a pastime or a hobby and should never be viewed as such. It is a serious enterprise in which only those who keep their eyes on the prize will eventually win out. The following five money keys are based on the experiences of a multitude of successful entrepreneurs. Read them carefully, it's some of the best advice you'll ever get.

THE FIVE MONEY KEYS

$ Money Key

Number 1 *The Successful Small Business Operator Has a Desire to Make Money!*

We've noted that the successful small businessperson must love to make money. But this is a different characteristic, this is the *desire* to make money. Four factors come into play when making this desire a reality: understanding the costs of doing business; making sure relationships with family and friends to not interfere with your business; and focusing your marketing efforts where it will help you the most.

The Costs of Doing Business

In order to make the money you desire, you must understand all the costs of doing business. For example, what are the total costs for a wholesale produce business? Include more than just the costs of the fruits and vegetables; include all of the other costs and expenses as well:

- Shipping both incoming and outgoing
- Warehousing
- Utilities for cold storage, telephone, heat, light and water
- Labor
- Selling expense
- Spoilage
- Packaging
- Insurance
- Bookkeeping
- Outside services such as legal and accounting
- Advertising
- and the list can go on and on.

Therefore, if you are in the wholesale produce business, you simply cannot look at only the cost of the produce you are purchasing for resale in order to set your selling price. Equally important, you must add something into the selling price for all of their other costs.

Relationship to Family and Friends

A second factor involved in the desire to make money is your relationship to family and friends. If you are to be successful in business, you have to treat the business as a business. For example, let us assume that, you have a clothing store. When a friend comes in to your store this does not automatically qualify her to make her purchase at cost or, at a substantial discount. You can't afford to treat family or friends any differently than any other customer. Don't "give away the store" just to be a nice guy. Yes, you may extend a courtesy discount. But, if every friend and relative was given extraordinary consideration, you are not going to be in business very long.

43

The same rule holds true for hiring new employees. Your personnel policy should be that you want to hire the most qualified individual at the most competitive salary. Jobs should not automatically go to relatives or friends unless you feel that they are genuinely capable. Treat the business as a business when you extend courtesy discounts, when you hire employees and in one other area-advertising

Marketing

The purpose of marketing is to bring customers into your place of business, to give you the opportunity to make a sale. Marketing costs money. It is an expense and an investment. Therefore, you must be sure to treat your marketing efforts like any other purchase you make for your business.

If a church member comes to your place of business and says, "Will you please purchase an ad in our church program? After all, it is your duty as a member of the church! "You don't automatically say yes. Likewise, students from a local school may ask you to purchase an advertisement for their school sports programs. Again, simply because your place of business is close to the school, or your child may have attend the school, or you know one of the teachers, doesn't mean that you automatically place an advertisement in the sports program.

Ask yourself certain questions. Will the ad or marketing program bring in customers? What will the advertisement produce in the way of business for your firm? Who will the advertisement reach? Is the goodwill generated by my supporting the church or the school going to bring in more business? Are the church members, students, faculty or parents customers or potential customers for my business?

If your answers to these questions indicate that advertising in the high school sports program will do nothing or little for your business, then don't place an advertisement in it. However, if you do advertise in it and if you spend your

44

advertising dollars in all of these "good will activities", don't look back later and wonder what happened to your advertising program? Don't say, "I spent all that money on advertising and got nothing out of it, so I am not going to advertise any more!" Using this kind of logic or coming to this conclusion is faulty and doing your business a terrible disservice.

On the other hand, if you want to make a contribution to the church or to the school, that's something else. Don't confuse your charitable contributions with legitimate business expenses. Advertising is an expense item for any business. Treat it like any other expense. Analyze it, study it, and be sure to purchase your advertising just like you would with any other item. That is, you want to receive the best buy for each dollar of expenditure or cost.

$ Money Key

Number 2   *The Successful Small Businessperson Knows All about the Features and Benefits of the Products or Services He or She Sells!*

In order to be successful, a small businessperson must be a complete expert on the product or service he or she is selling. For example, assume you are in the retail appliance business and you are selling television sets. A customer comes into your store looking for a 52" color TV set.

Why should the customer buy your product instead of someone else's? What are the features? Say, yours can show up to 10 channels on the screen at once. Or, it may have an automatic color system that maintains a perfect picture better than the competition's. And it may have built in super sound system. These features represent valuable benefits for the customer.

Being able to show multiple channels on the screen helps the user decide which to watch and helps assure that no attraction is being missed. The automatic color system adds value to this particular set. Finally, the super sound system adds to the enjoyment to the shows, especially films that have superior music and sound tracks.

Other dealers probably carry the same TV set, so your challenge is to give your customer a good reason to buy from you. That's called salesmanship. It's often been said that a good salesperson doesn't sell the steak, he or she sells the sizzle. But before you can sell that sizzle you have to be an expert on the products you are selling, the kind of services you can provide - and your costs of doing business. In the appliance business today, for example, the only profit a store makes can be in selling a long-term warranty at extra cost.

You may offer dollar savings to the customer, but you can't afford to sell products or services for less than your total cost of sales or without realizing a profit. It's one thing or the other, knowledge and salesmanship, lower prices or a reputation for superior service. You also have to know what your competition is doing and all the financial angles of buying, selling and stocking. In business, ignorance is not bliss, it can be fatal.

$ Money Key

Number 3   *The Successful Small Businessperson Knows How To Get Money From The Customer's Pocket Into His or Her Pocket!*

To accomplish this, you have to know your market. Who are your customers and prospects? Not necessarily by name and address. But how do you define them. Are they women, men, teenagers, senior citizens; or do they

2007 © Copyright American Institute of Small Business

represent a cross section of all ages. How big is your market? How many customers and prospects are in your market? What is your trading area or, the geographic boundaries of your customer base?

If you are in the wholesale supply business, what types of businesses will purchase from you? All businesses? Metal manufacturers? Automobile dealerships? Just how are your customers defined?

Once the market is defined, the successful small businessperson must attract these customers and prospects to his or her place of business. What type of advertising appeals to your prospective customer? Which media or forms of advertising: television, newspapers, direct mail, radio, or billboards? What type of advertising themes: hard sell, soft sell, prestige advertising or price busting, repetitive advertising or sensational, ever-changing themes? How frequently do you advertise?

Know what appeals most to your customers and prospects. What are their "hot buttons"? What brings them to you rather then to a competitor? Above all, once your customer's attention, how do you get them to take money from their pocket and put it into yours?

$ Money Key

Number 4   *The Successful Small Businessperson Knows How Their Leading and Most Successful Competition Makes Their Money!*

A wise old sage once said, "We never invent the wheel, we simply reinvent it." That is very smart advice. Who says that we have to be totally creative in order to be successful? Why not look at the number one competitor in our area and either come as close to them as possible, copy them, or go one step better?

Look at McDonalds. They were early in the field of fast food and now they are the biggest. But were they the first? No. What about the old White Tower and White Castle Hamburger shops. A & W Root Beer, Toddle House, and the list could go on and on.

Ray Kroc, the founder of McDonalds simply copied them and went several steps further. Then look what happened. Wendy's, Burger King, Arby's, Jack in the Box and more came into the field with various levels of success. They simply copied one another, added a new twist here and there, and off and took off.

So if you want to be successful, look at your competition.
- Where are they located?
- How do they advertise?
- What services do they offer? Gift Wrap, delivery, charge accounts, repair services and so on.
- What hours are they open?
- What days of the week are they open?
- What product lines do they carry?
- If they are a service operation, what are their rates?
- What lines do they carry?
- What color, sizes, shapes do they offer?
- How big of an inventory do they have?
- How do they sell?
- Who are their key personnel?

To be a successful small business operator, you need to know almost as much about your competition as you do about yourself. This is not always easy. But it is simply amazing what you can find out about your competition if you set

48

your mind to it. The important point being that if you can model your own business after a most successful competitor, your likelihood of success is greatly enhanced.

$ Money Key

Number 5   *The Successful Small Businessperson Knows How To Find and Use Someone Else's Money In Order To Make Money*!

Learning how to operate or start up your business on someone else's money is one of the most important lessons you'll learn in this book! It doesn't mean that you can go into or maintain a business without having to put in a single dollar. Yes, if you are going to start up a business, it's almost certain that you are going to have to use some of your own money. It may come from investments, savings, life insurance, a home equity loan or from the sale of some of your personal assets. But most likely, you do not have all of the necessary money to cover all the costs of starting a business. Or if the business is in full operation, there probably will come a time when you will need additional financing and will have to go out and get it.

Access to an unlimited source of operating funds is granted only to the federal government and a relative few, highly successful corporations. The rest of us do not have the luxury of having sufficient funds to start up a business or maintain one when times get tough.

A second luxury that most small businesspeople don't have is a business whose cash flow will generate immediate and continuing funds to start up or maintain business operations and growth. How wonderful it would be if we had a business that generated immediate cash to pay all of the start-up and operating expenses.

This means that we have to find a ready-made source of supply for your business's financial needs. The successful small business operator is acutely aware of this; usually the more successful a businessperson is, the more he or she knows about obtaining the necessary money for the business.

Money is available from a wide variety of sources: friends, relatives, loan companies, banks, customers, suppliers, the Small Business Administration, foundations, credit unions and insurance companies, among others.

Before exploring these many options, it's a good idea to examine yourself and your attitude toward money. That attitude must be positive with a capital *P*.

SKILLS INVENTORY

Following is a list of questions you might ask yourself to determine if you're right for a small business, or if a small business is right for you. By addressing your personal background, experience, aptitude, personal and business goals in this manner, you can realistically estimate your chances for success and can determine ways to sharpen your sharpen your approach to business matters. You'll better understand your abilities, weaknesses and the real person you are. You will identify your actual business goals, whether independence, money, business size, travel, people relations, status or something else. You'll get a better understanding of your personal goals, whether self-realization, creative expression, family, spirituality, physical health, or self-esteem.

Personal Attributes

1. Did you learn valuable lessons from businesses type activities in your childhood or teens?

2. Have you ever been fired from a job because of friction with or competition with

your boss or upper management?

3. How would you rate yourself on these characteristics?

Desire to make money	__Good	__Average	__Poor
Hard Worker	__Good	__Average	__Poor
Special Talents	__Good	__Average	__Poor
Success oriented	__Good	__Average	__Poor
Sociable	__Good	__Average	__Poor
Organized	__Good	__Average	__Poor
Competitive	__Good	__Average	__Poor

4. Why do you want to go into business for yourself? Consider practical, measurable reasons and personal reasons.

5. In what ways do you expect your new business to change your life during the first year?

6. How persistent are you?

7. How interested are you in solving problems?

8. How good are you with details and keeping yourself organized?

9. Do you have success-oriented habits?

> Are you early to bed, early to rise?
>
> Do you keep yourself physically fit?
>
> Are your personal finances, always accurate or often behind and overdrawn?
>
> Are you careful about your personal appearance?
>
> Are you careful about keeping appointments, and promises?
>
> Are you always on time for meetings?

10. Do you generally like people or prefer to be alone?

11. Are you a steady worker or need a push from time to time?

Business Qualifications

1. What skills do you have that would help in your business?

2. What experience do you have that could be applied to your business?

3. Will your hobbies and interests be an asset to the business?

4. What abilities have you acquired from schools, seminars, and training?

5. Make a list of things you are confident you are good at. Think about your school, work, community, and home experiences. List things you have done well; for example, you might have organized a fund drive, finished a recreation room, or coached a Little League team.

6. Make another list of the skills you have developed over the years. Examples might include: I am a good salesperson; I can examine the facts and make sound decisions.

7. List your personal strengths. Examples might include: I am dependable; I am understanding.

8. List personal weaknesses you would like to improve. Examples might include: I am impatient; I am often late for appointments.

9. Prepare a list of the activities you do now or will do for your business. List the major items, such as producing the product or rendering the service, invoicing, paying bills, answering the phone, making sales calls and so on.

What all entrepreneurs have in common is that they're looking for the kind of independence and freedom that's possible only through business ownership. While this is a fine goal, it involves a wide range of problems you may never event think about when you are working for a salary.

Chapter 5

What is Your Money Attitude?

You've thought long and hard about your business venture. You've done the research. You know exactly what you want to do and how you want to do it. You know what you're going to sell and how you're going to sell it. The next big step will be to get the money you'll need to turn those plans into reality. Before we go any further, however, it's important to take some time out to consider your attitudes about money and to understand some of the realities of borrowing.

Unless you have all the money you need, or a well-off and generous family, chances are you're going to have to use professional funding sources to get money to operate your business. Lenders and investors don't usually hand out money just because they like you or are impressed with the logic of your business idea. The golden rule in business is, he or she who has the gold makes the rules. If you go into the money market with unrealistic attitudes about money and the people who lend it, you're in for some disappointments and frustration.

This chapter will address some of the misunderstandings too many people have about money and borrowing. We'll also talk about the problems that face the loan providers you will contact, and how they operate.

WHAT IS MONEY?

If you think of money as something you use to buy goods or services, you're only partially correct. Money is also one way we keep track of our accomplishments. Consider the millionaires who continue to work day in and day out, long after they have all the money they'll ever need. They're typical of the way people often grade themselves and others by the bottom line on a financial statement.

It's important to understand your own attitude toward money before you make a loan request. Are you out to build a business, ensure financial success, or prove your ability to gain dollars just to be rich and influential? Your answer to this question can help or hinder the way you conduct your search for financing. The only practical way to obtain financing is to view the process objectively. This is a business arrangement, pure and simple.

COMMON MISCONCEPTIONS

If you think of lenders as narrow-minded bureaucrats whose only interest is digging into your personal life and whose only pleasure results from defeating your dreams, think again. For example, do you share any of these mistaken beliefs?

- Being in debt is bad business.

- A good personal credit rating should make business borrowing easy.
- Financial information should be kept secret.
- Business debts should have nothing to do with personal funds.
- Lenders should appreciate that business is unpredictable.
- Bankers get too involved in other people's business.
- Lenders have no imagination; they can't recognize a good idea.
- Nobody tells lenders the truth
- Banks lend money only to people who don't need it.

Anyone who has ever applied for a loan might find these and the following attitudes a little strange. Bankers have heard them all. We will consider these feelings and see how they can keep you from getting a loan.

Being in Debt Is Bad Business

It's a good rule to be careful with money, but there are times when it will be necessary to borrow funds. Think of money as a tool that helps your business reach its goals. Not borrowing money when it is needed, and can be safely paid back, is as foolish as borrowing too much money that can't be repaid.

A Good Personal Credit Rating Should Make
Business Borrowing Easy

You'd like to believe that your personal record for repaying loans should be enough to qualify you for a business loan. You know that you'll always pay back a loan; you always have.

A business loan is different. It is generally for a larger amount than any individual could easily repay. A business loan has to be paid back by the business. If your company can't produce enough to pay the loan, the bank will not get its money, even if the people who own the business honestly intend to pay their bills. That's why you will have to show the lender how the business is going to repay its loan. It's important to realize that in order to break even, a bank must make 97 good loans to make up for one bad loan.

Financial Information Should Be Kept Secret

When you borrow money the lender in a sense becomes your business partner. The lender needs to understand your financial status. Any lending institution needs to know what you are doing with your money to evaluate the likelihood of its being repaid. Your banker can be trusted with your personal and business financial information. If you ever doubt this, get a new banker, but never withhold information that the banker needs to properly analyze your loan request.

The owners of older, more established businesses may feel the company has proven itself and does not need such invasions of privacy. Don't let this become a part of your thinking. A banker can't do the best job for you and your company if he or she doesn't have all the needed financial tools.

Business Debts Should Have Nothing To Do With Personal Funds

One test lenders use is to see if you believe in your company enough to risk all or part of your personal assets. They could decide that if you don't have enough confidence to guarantee the debt, you should not be borrowing the money. Some large and well-fixed companies can borrow money without personal guarantees but smaller organizations often have to pass this test of confidence.

Lenders Should Appreciate That Business Is Unpredictable

No one has the foresight to accurately predict the future, but that doesn't mean you can't make a businesslike forecast about how your company will develop. If you don't at least make a try, you can't expect a lender to get an idea of how you will pay the loan back. It's your responsibility to put together appropriate plans and share them with your banker. Even if your first plan doesn't pan out, with experience, you'll soon get better at forecasting.

Bankers Get Too Involved In Other People's Business

Some people are afraid their lender will take control of their company's success or failure. A good banker can often make a difference in how a company develops, but contribute fully if you're not willing to share information. You have half the responsibility of creating an open and clear connection. At the same time, you are always free to accept suggestions or reject them. Bankers are in the business of making good loans and they are always out to make the best loan record they can.

Lenders Can't Recognize A Good Idea

You'll never know unless you ask. If you don't have confidence in your company and your loan request, it will be difficult for the lender to have confidence in you. If you have a good business idea, act with confidence, explain your case and ask for the loan. Don't risk leaving the lender in the dark as to whether you really wanted financing or were just fishing for information.

Lenders do not know everything about every industry. Use your business plan to educate them about your business and the benefits it will provide to your customers.

Nobody Tells Lenders The Truth

Getting financing is important, but establishing an ongoing business relationship is just as important. You never know when you'll have to go back to the well for more money. Being truthful with the lender, repaying your loans and fulfilling all your commitments will help to establish your business credit rating not only with your initial lender but for any financial dealings you'll have in the years to come. Trust creates the basic setting in which all business is conducted. Lenders and suppliers need to know that you are a dependable person with whom they will want to do business.

Banks Lend Money Only To People Who Don't Need It

This misconception is based on the fact that financial institutions want to be sure that borrowers have the means to repay their loans. They cannot afford to hand out money without a reasonable expectation that they'll get their money back and make a profit on the transaction.

Your responsibility is to convince the lender that your business is one that can and will pay back its loan. On any day in the United States, hundreds of billions of dollars remain outstanding in business loans. People who don't need money don't take out loans, so obviously plenty of businesses that need financial help and are getting it.

WHAT THE LENDER THINKS

Lending institutions are in the business of making loans, which they expect to be paid back and be profitable for them. They want to make loans and they really do try to accommodate their customers. At the same time, they have to be careful about whom they lend money to and how they do it. Compare lending to a business that sells a product and consider how company owners would feel about not getting paid for the products they sell. In addition, lenders have the added responsibility to pay the people who are "lending" the bank the money, which is the checking and saving account holders.

Lenders want to lend you money if they can see their way clear to doing it safely. Unfortunately, this is not always the case. There are other concerns that affect a banker's judgment.

A Loan Proposal Must Be Convincing

If the banker grants a loan, a lengthy process begins in which his or her reputation, judgment, and, perhaps job, will be put on the line.

The lender must review the loan request carefully; prepare a write-up for a loan committee or loan supervisor, and support the loan request under close questioning from bosses and associates.

Next, he or she must prepare the loan documentation and the necessary reports. The loan officer has to follow up after the loan is made and take action if collection might be necessary. The loan officer has to explain and defend the loan if any problems develop.

You can see why it is easier, and often safer, for a loan officer to simply turn down a loan. On the other hand, a loan officer who doesn't make loans will not have a job for long. A good loan proposal must convince lenders that it is in their interest to lend money to you.

A Loan Rejection Is Not A Personal Insult

Attitudes toward borrowing and lending affect a company's success in obtaining proper financing. Your challenge is to recognize and overcome your negative attitudes and misconceptions about money and borrowing. Then, with a good loan proposal, you can overcome any negative feelings the lender might have.

When a lender refuses to make a particular loan, the reason usually is that there are sound reasons to believe the loan will be a poor risk. A loan refusal is only one lender's estimate of the uncertainty involved in that loan request. It is not a judgment of your worth as a person.

Don't let your fear of rejection stand in the way of getting proper financing. If you make a habit of taking a loan refusal as a personal insult you can get into a mind-set that will make it difficult to obtain a loan anywhere. If you approach a lender with a resentful attitude, the lender may think that you don't have the open-minded attitude needed to run a business. That's strike one against

59

you.

You get a second strike if you approach a potential lender with the attitude that you will probably be turned down because you were refused by a lender before. Be positive: Every loan application is a new beginning. Every newly approached lender gives you a fresh opportunity to make your case better. Learn the lessons or your previous rejections and do not to repeat them.

One mistake some inexperienced people make is to try to feel out a lender without actually asking for the loan. If you hide your needs behind statements such as: "I don't really need the money, but would you lend it to me if I asked?" or "What is your bank's attitude toward first-time business loans?" you're fooling no one but yourself. Playing games with bankers, who really are practical businesspeople, is poison to the process.

Chapter **6**

The Secret To Easy Money

Every business owner wants their funding sources to embrace their business idea. They also want funding to come easily. There is one factor that is more important than any other factor. That factor is your credit history, judged mainly by your credit scores.

Credit scores are increasing in popularity as the largest factor business lenders look at when making a lending decision. And because of this, it is important that you understand the credit scoring industry.

A Brief History

Credit scoring was originally created over 100 years ago. Small retail merchants pulled their customer's financial information together to determine whether their customers were a good risk. The merchant associations developed into small credit bureaus. During the 1960's, problems starting arising because the reports were being used to deny services. The negative reports starting containing information not only about the customer's financial history but

61

also the individual's personal history from newspapers, such as sexual orientation, drinking habits and cleanliness.

In 1971, Congress passed the Fair Credit Reporting Act (FCRA). The FCRA was meant to increase the protect privacy and promote accuracy in the reports. Individuals also gained the right to view the reports, dispute and correct their information. In the end, positive financial history was also added.

It wasn't until George W. Bush signed an updated version of the FCRA in December 2003 that allowed consumers to view their credit scores for a reasonable fee. You can get your FICO score at www.myfico.com for around $50 or you can get a copy of your credit reports without your FICO score at www.annualcreditreport.com or by calling 877-322-8228.

Importance Of Your Credit

The information contained on your credit report directly impacts your overall credit score. In a 2004 study by the consumer protection group, U.S. Public Interest Research Group (US PIRG), almost 79% of all consumer credit reports have errors. Of those, about 25% had errors that would cause a denial of credit. More than half of the information contained on the reports was either outdated or belonged to someone else.

Before you approach a lender for financing, get a copy of your credit report. Look at this example of how credit score can affect the interest rate you receive on a $50,000 loan for 3 years.

	FICO Score	Interest Rate	Monthly Payment	Total Payments
Borrower 1	760-850	7.125%	$1,547	$55,692
Borrower 2	660-689	9.442%	$1,600	$57,600
Borrower 3	500-589	15.134%	$1,737	$62,532

As you can see, if you lender made a decision based entirely on credit score, you would be paying much more if you had a poor credit score compared to a good credit score, actually over $6,840 more in interest over a 3 year loan. In addition, credit scores under 640, normally will have an incredibly difficult time getting a loan.

Impact on Your Business Loan

Business lending has changed dramatically in the last few years. Over 20 years ago, many bankers would use the 4 C's of Credit to determine the risk of the borrower. The 4 C's of Credit are:

1. Character – Subjective judgment based on honesty, integrity and ethics
2. Capacity – The ability for the business or person to repay the loan
3. Capital – Financial Resources of the business based on the financial statements
4. Conditions – Reference to the external conditions surrounding the business

In the past, a lender would sit with you and understand your circumstances and your history to make an intuitive judgment if you were a good credit risk. Even though you may have had recent financial troubles, they would look at your current situation. Character was a major factor when being considered for a loan. Now, depending on the size of the lender and the region of the country, you may be judged by your credit score more than your character.

Smaller banks and banks in rural areas still depend heavily on character assessments as criteria for loan decisions. Larger banks are moving towards credit scores, not only as an annual audit, but as criteria for approvals.

Improving Your Credit Report

The first action you must take is to get a copy of your current

63

credit reports. Remember, you can get one for free annually at www.annualcreditreport.com.

Be sure to read over each item. Look for:

- Incorrect information
- Missing credit limits on your revolving balances (credit cards)
- Paid off items that don't show paid off, but were in reality paid off
- Alias names that are not yours
- Current creditors are listed and not the old ones (sometimes accounts are sold, but the old company shows the balances as unpaid and the new company shows the actual balances)

The items with the most impact to your score are (in order of importance):

1. Bankruptcy
2. Foreclosure
3. Repossession
4. Loan Default
5. Court Judgments

6. Collections
7. Past due payments
8. Late Payments
9. Credit Rejections
10. Credit Inquiries

Repairing Your Credit

Credit repair has become a big business. Be careful of companies promising to fix your credit in a short time period. The laws and regulations are very specific on how long each party has to respond to claims. Here is the basic process to repair your credit:

1. Get a copy of your report
2. Analyze the current credit report
3. Create a list of items that you would like to dispute
4. Write your letters of dispute and send them to the credit agencies and the creditor listed
5. DOCUMENT your efforts. This step is very important.
6. Analyze the results of the credit bureaus responses

64

Future Repair

Even though you may have poor credit, there are things you can do going forward to fix it easily. Look at these following steps:

- Pay your bills on time (especially your mortgage)
- Keep your credit card balance low compared to the maximum available to you
- A good history is critical, so do not close unused accounts – even zero balance accounts is a positive on your credit report
- Only apply for credit when you need it or you are getting a better rate – be sure to read the fine print to ensure it is a better rate than any other option you already have.
- Separate accounts after a divorce
- Avoid excess inquiries into your credit history. If you apply for multiple credit cards at once, it will lower your credit score. A lot of inquiries in a short period of time will have a negative impact on your credit.
- Avoid Bankruptcy – bankruptcy can take up to 7 years to leave your credit report. Bankruptcy should be the very last resort you consider.
- Negotiate with your creditors – before you fall behind on payments, call the creditor to see if there are other options available. Working with the creditor in an arrangement that works for both of you can help your credit report also. Creditors may be able to offer you reduced interest rates, ability to skip payments, reduce late fees and finance changes or lower your minimum monthly payments.

In the beginning of any business it is beneficial to get the lowest rate on your funding. With more and more lenders moving towards credit scores as a standard for loan approvals, it is becoming increasing important for you to understand and manage your credit scores and reports.

Chapter 7

Business

Planning

There are many reasons for preparing a business plan; each in itself is sufficient for getting the job done before you proceed any farther in the process of starting or expanding your business. Regardless of the specific reason, however, the underlying goal of preparing a business plan is to ensure the success of the business.

A properly developed business plan provides more than mere numbers on paper. It serves these main functions:

1.   To provide you with the ROAD MAP that you need in order to run your business. It allows you to make detours, change directions, and alter the pace that you set in starting or running the business.

2.   To assist you in financing. Whether one is starting up a small business or is an entrepreneur, banks and financial institutions want to see that you know where you are, where you are going, and how you are going to get there.

3. The plan will tell you how much money you need, when you will need it, and how you are going to get it. In other words, how you will do your financing?

4. To help you clearly think through what type of business you are starting, and allows you to consider every aspect of that business.

5. To raise the questions that you need to have answered in order to succeed in your business.

6. To establish a system of checks and balances for your business so that you avoid mistakes.

7. To set up bench marks to keep your business under control.

8. To help you develop the COMPETITIVE SPIRIT to make you keenly prepared and ready to operate.

9. To make you think through the entire business process so that you do not open the business blindly or lack vital information in opening and maintaining your business.

10. To force you to analyze competition.

11. It will give you a "GO" or "NO GO" ANSWER about starting the business.

If these functions don't convince you that you need a business plan, we have a suggestion: Ask any business person who has failed whether or not they had prepared a business plan ahead of time.

Sure, it takes time, effort and maybe even money to prepare a document like this. But if it can make the difference between success and failure, it's worth it. So, let's get started.

HOW TO PREPARE YOUR BUSINESS PLAN

First, decide right now that your business plan will be neat and well-written. Its final appearance will have a significant effect on others who read it. Therefore, if you are weak in the areas of writing, hire someone to help with the final preparation.

Your plan is a reflection of you and your ability to organize, to think, to manage and to communicate. In the eyes of a financing source -- one who may invest his or her money in your new enterprise -- it demonstrates on paper your potential ability to compete in the business arena. If your plan is sloppy, with spelling and grammatical errors, the financing source may determine that if you write that way,

68

you may not run your business well.

No two business plans will be alike. The one thing to keep in mind as you write you business plan is: Would you give money to the owners of this business? How do you show that your hair salon is going to be more profitable than the one down the street?

If raising money is the primary purpose of your plan, you can readily understand its importance to you. Treat it accordingly. It **must** be well organized, easy to read, sound, logical and factual. Investors must see the direct relationship between **future growth** and past **knowledge** and **experience**. The "blossoms" of tomorrow will be the natural fulfillment of the "seeds" you plant today.

Your business plan is not written in stone. You will probably discover its need for fine-tuning at brief intervals at first. And, certainly, if your initial requests for capital are rejected, you should take another look at it. The idea is to make this document serve **your** needs.

If you have done your homework and the result is an idea that has merit, there is a good chance that someone or some group will want to support you financially. Most good plans can find funding with the right financing source. Once you sell your idea, it will be up to you to implement the plan and continue planning for growth.

BUSINESS PLAN OUTLINE

There are many different forms of business plans. Each industry and business has its own type and format, but the following outline is used by many, many financing sources and banks around the country. It is very important to have your business plan in a format the bankers are familiar with. It shows that you have thought through all the pieces of your business.

I.	Cover Sheet and Table of Contents
II.	Executive Summary
III.	Company Information
IV.	Industry, Market and Competition
V.	Products and Services

EXECUTIVE SUMMARY

The executive summary is your first place to make a good impression on the reader, but normally this is the last section written. Some financing sources will only read the Executive Summary to see if they are interested in the business concept. The page should start with your business name, your name and title, business address and phone number. It should also be no more than 2 pages. The Executive Summary should include the following topics which are summaries from the other parts of your plan:

A. Mission Statement

What is your purpose and goal for the business? What do you think the business will look like when you are finished building it. A Mission Statement should be no longer than 5 sentences long.

B. Summary of the Description of the Business

Will yours be a sole proprietorship? A partnership? Corporation? In this section, you should cover the nature of your business (i.e. restaurant, bakery, catering, or farming). In addition talk about the type of business you are thinking about (manufacturing, services, wholesale, retail or other). Briefly describe your products and/or services and who your customers will be and how you will sell to them (i.e. walk-in, stores, telephone sales, mail order). Discuss the quality of products and services and an estimate of prices.

If your company is new, state it. If it is an existing business or you are purchasing a business, briefly discuss the history of the business and your philosophy to expand it.

C. Industry, Market and Competition

Explain the big picture first. What is the total universe of your market? Is the

70

industry growing or declining? Is anything happening now or expected to happen in the future that will impact your business? Who are your competitors? How successful are they, and why? Do they have any weaknesses? If so, will your business fill a need created by their weakness? Who will your customers be? Why will they buy your product or service?

D. Products and Services

You will need to provide a complete description of what you plan to sell or rent. Emphasize the basic product or service that will provide the bulk of your income. Explain advantages and benefits and anything about your products or services that will help "sell" your business concept to a complete stranger. If your product is still on the drawing board, explain when it will be available, including any test data you have.

Describe how your product or service will be sold. Include pricing strategy, estimated sales and market share for each of the first three years. Add your advertising and public relations plans, plus your service and warranty policies.

E. Supplier and Operations

Cover all the specifics, such as how, where and by whom your product will be produced. What is the raw material? Is it readily available? What is the manufacturing process? What is your anticipated rate of   production? Will you use union or non-union labor? Who are your major suppliers?

F. Marketing Plan

Your marketing plan is going to cover the specifics of Product, Price, Place, Promotion and Persuasion. Also included will be your advertising, public relations and publicity strategy and goals. In this section, talk about the different types of media your will use and why.

G. Management Team

How many people are involved, and what are their skills? How well are they qualified? At what points in time will you add personnel? If you're running a one-man show, explain convincingly how you have the necessary skills and talent to achieve your goals.

H. Financial Considerations

If yours is a new business, you won't have the benefit of past history. As a bare minimum, you will need a personal financial statement. If your business is already established, include a financial statement for the business. Demonstrate how you plan to elevate existing figures from point A to point B. Ideally, you will be totally familiar with all of the financial details of your business, and will be able to answer -- line-by-line -- how you arrived at each figure.

Include summary Profit and loss projections for 3 years and an expected balance sheet at the end of each year.

Be careful not to make you executive summary too long. It should stick to 1-3 pages. Focus on the opportunity in this part of the plan. The rest of the items will be discussed in further detail later in the plan.

COMPANY AND LOCATION

The Company part of your business plan should talk about the past and the future of your business. If you are an existing business or you are purchasing a company discuss how the company did historically and how you intend to improve. Include when the company was founded, what financing has been used, what does the organization look like, and if buying a company, why the current owners want to sell the business.

After discussing the history, describe the current status of the organization. What are the strengths and weaknesses? Many owners can talk freely about their company's strengths. Many of the same owners will not discuss the potential weaknesses in their concept. It is important for you and your financial sources to understand the weaknesses and determine how to minimize them. Most people who will read your plan realize that ALL businesses have weaknesses.

Finally talk about the future. Describe your goals for the future. Try to quantify your goals. What will your sales be 1 year from now? 3 years? 5 years? How about profits? Can you match any of your projections to outside trends? Are clothing retailers increasing business because the population continues to grow where you live? Is the Census Bureau seeing the same trends continue? The objectives are more believable if you have an experienced management team with a history of setting and achieving their objectives.

Location

When writing about your location, describe the location and why you chose it. Refer back to the chapter in this book on Site Selection. Describe items like:

- Your trade area – where are your customers compared to where you are?
- Traffic patterns – Can customers get to your place easily?
- Complimentary businesses
- Competition location – Where are they compared to your location?
- Parking spaces for clients - Is it enough?
- Zoning restrictions – check with local city/town hall to make sure you can do business in this location
- Permits and Licenses – check with local city/town hall to make sure what permits you will need. For example, most cities will limit the size of the sign you can have in front of your business.
- Expansion room – Is there room if you need it?
- Blueprint of your store or office – How will everything look once you have it set up?

Be sure to mention if you plan to rent or lease or purchase your site. If you rent or lease, what are the terms of the lease. For example, how long is the lease, how much notice can you give to get out of the lease, what penalties, payment, and when can payment be increased.

In writing this part of your business plan, make sure it doesn't just repeat the information in the executive summary, but adds more detail to it.

INDUSTRY, MARKET & COMPETITION

Industry - Understanding your industry is very important. You would not want to start a business in making and selling personal computers with 486 computer chips. This would not be a business that would last very long. Even in the restaurant industry there are certain types of restaurants that are increasing in business while others are decreasing or closing. You need to focus on the how the industry is performing now and how it will continue to perform in the future. In the industry

73

section you should include research on:

Industry Size – How big is the pie? To determine the industry size talk to different people that are connected with the industry. These can be current business owners or trade associations. Estimate the industry size in annual dollars or units sold for the past few years. It is growing or shrinking? Although you may know a lot about the industry size and characteristics, the reader of your business plan may not know. Explain the industry at a national level and then try to bring the information to a local level.

Growth Rate – From the industry size you can determine at what rate it is growing and determine if the trend is to continue to grow or to become steady. Compare your company's growth rate with what you calculated for the industry. Are they alike?

Key Growth Factors – These are factors that are up and beyond the control of the industry or any company within the industry. There are factors that affect the industry's market size and level of demand. For example, the tragedy of September 11, 2001 strongly affected the travel and hotel industry. Both of these industries had decline factors that were beyond their control. It is important in this section, for your benefit, that you describe both positive and negative growth factors that may affect your business. It will help you develop a strategy for the different factors. Growth factors will include situations like the economic condition of the United States, trade relations between your suppliers and the countries where your products are produced or specific economic conditions of the city or town where you live.

Cyclical Features – Some industries have a pattern that happens every few years. For instance, the mortgage industry is very cyclical. Every few years the rates go up and then in a few years the rates go down. During the period where rates are down, more people can start businesses in the mortgage industry. Whereas if you try to start a mortgage company when the rates are up, it is much harder to do. Understand your industry to know when it may be a better time to start a business in that industry.

Seasonality – Many businesses may be seasonal, which means they have better sales in different parts of the year. For example, in Minnesota, boat sales do not do as well in the months of November to March. On the other hand, snowmobile sales are way

74

up during this time of year. Both businesses depend on the season for their sales. Garden Centers, bike shops, and outdoor restaurants are also seasonal businesses. Use this information to your advantage and start a business at the right time of year for the earliest success.

To find some of this information you can check with your local library and look for industry publications in the Business Periodicals Index. Other places to find information would be in general business publications like Forbes, Fortune or Business Week. Some of the information may be difficult to interpret as a small business. Therefore industry size and growth will need to be estimated.

Market

How big of a slice of pie are you targeting? Once you understand that the industry has total sales of $10 million, what percentage of that do you want for your business? You want to make sure there are enough customers to support your business. Start by looking at market or customer characteristics like: age, sex, ethnic group, education, family size, income, business type, and geographic location. You are trying to determine the most important characteristics that relate to your customers.

Competition

The goal of the competition portion of your business plan is to convince the reader that you know what you are up against. Refer back to the chapter on Site Selection for your research. Review your notes on the competitive analysis survey that you did on the competitors in your area and the map of the locations of your competitors. This will help you more easily describe who the competition is and what are their strengths and weaknesses. Be sure to include answers for the following points:

❖ Annual sales
❖ Location
❖ Strengths
❖ Weaknesses
❖ Product line depth & breath

❖ Pricing compared to yours
❖ Marketing activities
❖ Supply sources
❖ Expanding or declining
❖ Skilled employees

PRODUCTS AND SERVICES

The next parts of the plan will go into more detail about your products in your business. A sample outline would be:

> A. Initial Products and Services
> B. Proprietary Features
>> 1. Patents
>> 2. Copyrights
>> 3. Unique or different features
> C. Future Products and Services
>> 1. New products and services
>> 2. Research and development
>> 3. Expansion plans

Before you start writing for this section take a few minutes to think about your objectives. What level of quality are your products going to be, high, average or low quality? What price level are they going to sell at? At this point start to make a list of products or services that you would initially like to offer. Refer back to the Market Research chapter to see the answers you received on your questionnaires and surveys. Target products that customers were looking for and see if the pricing allows you to make a profit when selling it.

Secondly, almost all businesses have unique features for their products. Even in a standard flower shop, unique or secret features may include a special distributor for a specific flower or a new way creating special occasion flowers. It may even be a location that is convenient or added benefits when customers shop there.

Unique features can include things specific to your products, your store or office or your customer services. All these items together will make up your unique business. Think about Disney World. When someone goes to Disney World it is a destination. It is all about the experience. Can you make your place of business or the way you conduct business with your customers a better experience? Are you easy to do business with?

Next list the products you want to add in the future. These may be products

76

that are in research and development. They may be products that you want add to your product line that you currently do not have funding to carry. In expanding your product line are you going to add more products to the same market or are you going to increase your customers for your same products? Remember it is much easier and less expensive to sell to current customers than to find new ones.

Keeping your product line current and up-to-date is important to keep sales coming in the door. Make sure you continue to understand your customer's changing needs for products.

SUPPLIERS AND OPERATIONS

Suppliers.

Having reliable and cost effective suppliers is very important to a small business. You should include suppliers for the initial equipment and for ongoing supplies and raw materials. In this section, you can list major suppliers and backups if the major supplier can not deliver. You can discuss payment and delivery terms for each supplier. Buying on price may not always be a wise decision. Some suppliers may allow you to buy on credit or with extended payment terms.

Operations.

Production processes should be discussed in detail in this section. Include facility requirements, equipment requirements, and labor requirements. Explain how customer service will handle questions and problems from customers, how your networks and telephone will be maintained, how your software and hardware will be updated or how your shipping department will be managed. If you are manufacturing a product be sure to include flow of materials through your plant and other necessary processes.

You will also want to discuss briefly if you plan to buy your equipment or lease your equipment and from whom.

MARKETING PLAN

You should start this section with the goals for your marketing plan. These would include your marketing objectives and the measurements you plan to use to see if your advertising and promotional events are working up to your expectations. Refer to the Advertising and Publicity and Promotions chapters for more information.

The marketing part of your business plan should be a detailed plan of your promotion mix. Promotion Mix should include a breakdown of your advertising, sales promotions, personal selling, publicity and public relations events. Which one of these you choose depends on many factors on how much money you have to spend, what your competition uses, and how each one will meet your marketing goals. Your strategy should be a result from weighing the different options and your different goals.

It should include what type of media, the number of times you plan to use that media form, cost of media types, and who you are targeting with the media you chose. Make sure to include the reasons you chose the different media types and why you think they are going to be most effective.

A calendar is the best way to show when the different events or media publications will be used. You can also include the deadlines for submission to the different promotions. Try to schedule at least some event for each month. Also be sure to track results you are receiving from your different marketing programs.

Marketing Calendar

Activity	Jan	Feb	Mar	Apr	May	Jun	Jul	Aug	Sep	Oct
Grand Opening Publicity	X									
Grand Opening Event		X								
Special Offer Publicity		X								
Sponsor Block Party - Publicity					X					
Open House						X				
July 4 Sale - Publicity										
Photo Contest								X		
Winning Photos to Newspapers									X	

It is important in this section to focus on how you will get the edge on your competition and how you will win customers. This should be an action plan for your business. Continually refer back to your target market to make sure you are targeting the promotion to fulfill a customer's need.

Remember the most valuable asset in any business is its client list. It is therefore important to show how you will add customers to your list and how you plan to communicate and sell to them on an on-going basis.

The best way to add clients to your list is to have a process within your company to ask customers for their information. If you have customer who are reluctant to give out their information, offer them an incentive to become part of your mailing list, maybe a free gift or special introductory offer.

MANAGEMENT TEAM AND KEY PERSONEL

The management team is very important to the success of your business. It has been said that financing sources will "fund" a business with an "A" management team and a "B" idea before they will fund a "B" management team with an "A" idea. Keep in mind that not everyone on your management team will be receiving a paycheck. The management team can consist of advisors and other business professionals that you work with, including your banker, accountant, consultants and lawyer. This section should answer the following: "What qualifies the management team to run this type of business?" If you have one, include an organizational chart.

Next include a short paragraph on each person with management responsibilities. The write up should include information that directly relates to the current business you are starting or buying. For example, your Senior Marketing person should have not only experience in marketing for a small company, but also for your specific industry or a closely related industry.

Business advisors, consultants and other professionals should be included next. These individuals tend to bring experience and knowledge that other members of your management team may not posses. Business advisors can include a formal board of directors or an informal advisory board. Either should include someone with expertise in banking, law, accounting and marketing. It is incredibly helpful to have input from outside parties. Sometimes small business owners get caught up in the day to day activities and lose sight of the big picture. Outside advisors can help make sure this does not happen.

In addition to management, a short paragraph should be included for key personnel. For example, you were starting a home remodeling business and your mother has agreed to help you get started. You should include in this section that your mother has over 8 years working with Habitat for Humanity as a carpenter. Although she will not be active in the management of the business, her experience is invaluable.

Finally talk about the on-going personnel needs of your business. What do you see as the next employees that you will have to hire? Will it be easy to find those individuals with the experience you are looking for? What is your final plan for number of employees? 5 employees? Or 100 employees? Does the future personnel needs match the other growth projections? Do you have access to a qualified pool of employees around your place of business?

FINANCIAL PLAN

The financial plan should be the last piece you create before the Executive Summary. Review the chapters on Finding Money and Beginning Bookkeeping. These will help you to create the plan for your specific business. The financial plan should include the following plans:

Summary of Financials
Sources and Uses of initial funding
Balance Sheets for 3 years
Income Statements for 3 years
Cash Flow Statements for 3 years

All of the financial plans should be in the common form known to financing sources. Most of these people look at dozens of financial statements a day, so making them look different will only make you look like you do not know what you are doing in the financial area.

If you have an existing business, cover the past financial performance of the business. You should use those numbers to calculate the future. You can not make the assumption that you will grow by 100% over the next three years, when in the past you have grown by only 5%, without some reasons.

Explain your assumptions. The reader may not be familiar with your industry.

If you are estimating expenses, explain how you can to that number.

Summary of Financials

The summary of financials should include the profit or loss projections for the next three years, when positive cash flow is expected, net worth summary from the balance sheet for the next three years and any assumptions made in the financial statements.

Income Statement Summary

	Year 1	Year 2	Year 3
Sales	$100,000	$150,000	$200,000
Expenses	75,000	100,000	150,000
Profit	25,000	50,000	50,000

Cash flow is expected to turn to positive cash flow in 15 months from start date.

Balance Sheet Summary

	Year 1	Year 2	Year 3
Owner's Equity	$125,000	$150,000	$200,000

Sources and Uses Statement

This spreadsheet should contain where the monies are coming from and what are they being spent on. The following is an example:

SOURCES AND USES OF FUNDS

SOURCES

Anywhere State Bank

Commercial Loan, Anywhere State Bank	$50,000
Cash from the Ashford's Savings and	
sale of some of their common stock	$25,000
Total Sources	$75,000

USES	
Equipment Suppliers, Inc.	$20,000
Initial Food Inventory	$10,000
Working Capital	<u>$45,000</u>
Total Uses	$75,000

Balance Sheet Example

ED ENTREPRENEUR

BALANCE SHEET AS OF OCTOBER 31, 200X

ASSETS		LIABILITIES	
Cash in Bank	7,470	Accts Payable	
Accts Rec	1,000	Commission Payable	250
Inventory	350	**Total Liabilities**	250
		Capital Paid In	350
		May Earnings	900
		June Earnings	1,770
		July Earnings	500
		August Earnings	1,000
		September Earnings	1,775
		October Earnings	2,275
		Total Equity	8,570
Total Assets	**8,820**	**Total Liabilities & Owner's Equity**	**8,820**

Income Statement Example

ED ENTREPRENEUR

INCOME STATEMENT

OCTOBER 31, 200X

REVENUES:		
Sales of 50 widgets	5,000	
Less: Returns	0	
		$5,000
EXPENSES:		
Sales Commissions	500	
Cost of Goods Sold	600	
Tools	25	
Depreciation	400	
Building Rent	375	
Interest Expense	240	
Accounting Services	100	
Total Expense		2,240
Net Income		**2,760**

Cash Flow Statement Example

Projected Cash Flow Statement

For the Twelve Months Ended December 31, 20XX

	Apr	May	June	Jul	Aug	Sep
Sources of Cash:						
Sales	**2,500**	**3,000**	**3,500**	**500**	**500**	**1,000**
Uses of Cash:						
Cost of Sales	1,175	1,350	1,575	275	275	450
Operating Expenses	1,443	1,555	1,668	893	893	1,055
Total Uses:	**2,618**	**2,905**	**3,243**	**1,168**	**1,168**	**1,505**
Increase (Decrease)	(118)	95	257	(668)	(668)	(505)
Cumulative Cash Flow	**(118)**	**(23)**	**234**	**(434)**	**(1,102)**	**(1,607)**

	Oct	Nov	Dec	Jan	Feb	Mar
Sources of Cash:						
Sales	**1,000**	**6,000**	**6,000**	**12,000**	**6,000**	**6,000**
Uses of Cash:						
Cost of Sales	450	900	900	1,800	900	900
Operating Expenses	1,455	2,380	2,380	3,530	2,180	2,330
Total Uses:	**1,905**	**3,280**	**3,280**	**5,330**	**3,080**	**3,230**
Increase (Decrease)	(905)	2,720	2,770	6,670	2,920	2,770
Cumulative Cash Flow	**(2,512)**	**208**	**2,928**	**9,598**	**12,518**	**15,288**

APPENDICIES TO THE BUSINESS PLAN

The Appendix should include any other information that you feel is important that does not fit in another area of the business plan. This may include:

1.   Resumes of the management team
2.   Business policies regarding return policies, personnel policies or employee handbook
3.   Estimate on equipment that you would need to run your business
4.   Initial marketing campaign
5.   Potential lease agreement
6.   Partnership agreement
7.   Signed contracts for product
8.   Letters of recommendation from industry experts or potential clients

The really smart people, who do a lot of planning, say that about 85% of what's going to happen in your business can be anticipated; therefore, you can have a plan in place to deal with most situations. The remaining 15% are the crises, the things you absolutely have to address when they come up. With proper planning your business runs itself instead of running you, so you will have the time and patience you'll need to give proper attention to all the unforeseen problems that will pop up in even the best run business.

Chapter 8

Estimating Your Money Needs

Every start-up business or established company must determine its real financial needs. At first glance, it would seem that no company can have too much money; but even a good company can fail if it's short of funds. A business can also run into trouble if it has too much financing and has difficulty paying back loans.

What's most important is to determine the level of funding that will ensure proper operations without placing a strain on debt repayment. Before you can sensibly estimate how much money you will need, however, you have to know exactly what you plan to do. Think of any sort of business planning activity as an opportunity to ensure your business's success. Only by thinking through your business logically and systematically, from initial idea to final product or service, will you be able to realistically determine financial needs.

TWO TYPES OF FINANCING

Careful planning is the necessary ticket to successful financing or funding. In other words, it opens the door to reaching those people whose money you are going to use. Financing falls into two general categories: debt financing and equity financing.

Debt Financing

In its most elementary form debt financing, is simply taking out a loan from a funding source and paying interest on it. Let's consider the example of a bank loan. Whether for use as working capital, a building mortgage, purchase of inventory or raw material, financing of a new venture or the purchase of a company truck are examples of debt financing. The bank provides the money and charges the borrower interest for the use of that money.

Debt financing relies heavily upon the individual or company's ability to pay back a loan. This can be in the form of putting up collateral or making available to the loan source assets equal or close to the value of the loan. It's like an insurance policy for the lender. That way, if the borrower defaults, the bank or loan agency is protected against loss. For example, collateral can be a first or second mortgage on a building, inventory, raw material, stocks, bonds, insurance or any other form of asset that can be assigned.

Debt financing can also rely on the firm's or individual's history. In the case of established companies and individuals that have a good credit history and rating, their history can be based simply on their reputation, size or the perception of their business in the community.

Equity Financing

Equity financing means obtaining funds in exchange for selling or giving up a part of interest in the business. Equity financing is not a loan; rather, it is the sale of part of your business. The purchaser relies upon is his or her belief that buying into the business is a good investment.

Equity financing has become very popular in recent years, especially in the biomedical, computer software and hardware and other high tech product development fields. These companies often have a product concept for which development costs can be considerable. Because they do not have the net worth, collateral or ability to repay any type of loan, they sell a portion of their business to raise money. Shares can be sold to the general public and listed on a national or local stock exchange. Common stock can also be privately held by shareholders and not publicly traded.

CASH FLOW MANAGEMENT

To a small business, cash flow management is more than simply matching dollars in with dollars out. In fact, the way you manage cash can have a major impact on your profitability. One simple way to begin an analysis of your cash flow needs is to divide funds into three categories, each of which can be managed to enhance your bottom line:

1. Incoming funds
2. Outgoing funds
3. Static funds

Incoming Funds

These are the revenues that come into your business from sales made to customers either for cash or credit. Cash flow is the lifeblood of any business, so it=s crucial to keep that money flowing in, to maintain control of your cash receivables. Your profits can suffer when you have money tied up in past-due receivables.

A favorable cash flow statement can be a big help when you need to go to the bank to borrow funds.

Outgoing funds

These are the operating expenses that flow out of the business. They include accounts payable, salaries, taxes, and other items necessary to conduct your business. If current cash expenses are too high and putting a drain on cash, banks and others might look negatively on such a situation.

Static funds

These include the cash and inventory that you keep on hand. They add nothing to your bottom line. These can also include:

- Raw materials
- Consumables
- Fixed plant and equipment (buildings, forklift trucks, machinery, etc.)
- Office machines
- Office furniture
- Trucks and other vehicles

Static funds can be used to enhance your cash position. For example you can deposit your available cash in a safe interest-bearing account as funds come in, so there's no reason to let your cash sit idly.

BUDGETING

The core of your business planning is the cash budget, which translates operating plans into dollars. Without a cash budget, you have no way of estimating financial needs. Few investors or creditors will even consider a request for money without one.

The cash budget helps a lender answer these important questions:

- How much money do you need?
- How will you spend the money?
- How soon will you pay us back?

The entrepreneur who is put off by numbers misses their important role in the efficient operation of any business venture. An understanding of financial matters is as important to a venture's survival and growth as production, marketing and other basic business functions.

Because most small businesses don't have a lot of working capital, most must do without the services of a good accountant in start-up or expansion phases, when they can do the most good. Large corporations often have the luxury of hiring financial experts skilled in all aspects of the business.

Here's a tip: Instead of hiring your own personal accountant, contact the State Department of Economic Development Office, or the Small Business Development Center (SBDC) or the local SCORE office near you. Many of these centers have accounting experts who will help you develop your own accounting and recordkeeping systems. They can also help you work through any accounting problems that you might encounter. If you don't have a local SBDC, contact your nearest Small Business Administration Office for advice. All SBDCs, SCORE Offices and SBA offices are listed on the SBA's web site at www.sba.gov.

USES OF MONEY

Few people have difficulty spending money. Every entrepreneur, however, should be familiar with and prepared for some very important uses of money. Below are typical uses of money.

Working capital

This money is used to buy inventory, pay salespersons, make lease payments, web site costs and handle unexpected costs until your Incoming Funds (revenues) can pay for all the Outgoing Funds (expenses).

Inventory

Because inventory can consume large amounts of working capital, make sure you buy the right amount of inventory. In retailing, for example, too-small quantities may lead to empty shelves and lost customers. Too large a stock, on the other hand, can raise your costs due to excess inventory and obsolete merchandise.

Excess inventory is a nonworking asset. As long as it sits on shelves, inventory ties up cash while producing no return. If your inventory is financed, you're actually paying someone for your stock to gather dust. To reduce inventory, some companies are turning to "just-in-time" systems. Instead of overstocking raw materials to ensure fast delivery, a just-in-time system shifts the burden to vendors through contracts that guarantee rapid shipments to fulfill customer orders.

Capital Equipment Purchases

Whether you start a business, buy one or get into a franchise, some of your largest expenses will be for capital equipment. When building your budget, remember that loans for machinery and capital equipment are generally easier to get, because they are secured by the equipment as collateral. These types of loans are based on the life of the equipment, but generally not for more than ten years. Certain technology costs are considered capital equipment purchases, but typically only if they cost over $5,000.

Research and Development

Ideas are the basis for most businesses, large and small. One idea may be enough to start an enterprise, but it isn't enough to maintain growth. The importance of improving existing products and developing new ones has never been more evident than it is today. Here are just a few examples or research and development in today's marketplace: The Campbell's Soup Company never stops developing new varieties and uses for their soups; Microsoft constantly enhances and upgrades its product line; automobile companies are always involved in new product developments; even Hershey Chocolate eventually diversified into other candy products, building on the success of its original Hershey Bar to keep its share of an increasingly competitive market.

The lesson is that research and development is a continuing need for many businesses and that funds must be allocated or found for product development on a continuing basis.

Expansion

A good idea can't be held down. If a retailing idea is good in one location, two stores will probably be even better and ten stores will create a commanding purchasing situation. The same holds true in other marketing fields. If you've put together a hot selling organization for one line of products, chances are you can take on another line or two and be that much more successful.

Naturally, expansion always brings with it extra costs, but additional financing should be easy to come by if you have a successful record to show for your efforts.

Purchasing a Business

You never know when the opportunity to acquire a good company will come along, whether in your own business or in an allied field. Many entrepreneurs have made a career of going from success to success by keep keeping their eyes peeled for the right opportunity. Naturally, the better the record you establish in your main business, the easier it will be to get financing for a new acquisition.

CASH FLOW CONSIDERATIONS

Once you've established your business plans, it's time to set the facts and figures down on paper so you'll have a pretty good idea of how much money you'll need. Prospective lenders will definitely want to see some realistic figures before they even consider your request. They'll want to know how well you've budgeted your business as an indication of what kind of a risk (and rewards) you represent to them. In order to arrive at the right amount, you'll need to do some financial forecasting in the form of an income and expense forecast and cash flow projection.

Income and Expense Statement

It helps to think about the income and expense statement as the operating statement you would expect to see for your business at the end of a particular period, generally a year. For a new business, the forecast will be a prediction of revenues and expenses for the first year of operation. In either case, the analysis should answer the basic question of whether your business is going to make money. An example of an income and expense statement is shown in Figure 7.1.

Figure 7.1   Income and Expense Statement

AMERICAN PUBLISHING COMPANY

Year Ending December 31, 200X

INCOME	
20,000 books at $15.00 each	$300,000
EXPENSES	
Printing & Binding at $5.00 per book	$100,000
Wages and benefits for 2 employees	95,000
Depreciation on equipment	1,000
Overhead (power, light, heat, water)	2,000
Equipment repairs	500
Delivery & Freight	1,000
Marketing Expenses	1,500
Insurance	500
Rent	8,400
Interest on loans	200
Communications including Internet	2,400
Taxes	900
Accounting & Legal	800
Travel & Entertainment	2,000
Miscellaneous	1,200
TOTAL EXPENSES	**217,400**
NET PROFIT	**82,600**

Income

The first, and most uncertain, figure to estimate is income or sales. Because you need this figure to calculate your materials cost, you have to give your best estimate. Be conservative, it is better to underestimate than go overboard.

When estimating income, always keep in mind the following considerations:

- *Financing Costs*. If you use a line of credit to finance operations while waiting for your receivables to be paid, you are providing your clients with interest-free loans while paying interest to borrow against your line.

- *Opportunity Costs*. If you had the money in hand, you could be investing it - either to earn interest or to make your company grow. But until your invoices are paid, your return is zero.

- *Administrative Costs*. The longer a receivable stays on the books, the more you pay in rebilling costs, collection fees and related expenses.

To avoid such costs, you must establish an effective credit policy. Usually this includes methods for establishing and reviewing customer credit, service charges on over-due invoices, progress payments for products to be delivered over a period of time and positive collection efforts.

The most effective way to ensure timely payments is to keep in frequent and close contact with clients.

Expenses

Now prepare a list of expense items and your estimate of their costs-include such items as the following:

- *Labor*-This is the total amount of money you will be paying employees over the period of the statement.

- *Materials*-Depending on the type of business, this may include such items as office supplies, gift wrap, shipping supplies and so on.

- *Depreciation*-When you purchased any item that has a life span of three years or longer, the Internal Revenue Service normally will not allow you to

96

treat the total cost of the item as a one-year expense. Rather, you are required to divide the cost of the item by the average life in terms of years assigned to the item. Thus, if an item costing $3,000 has a life span of three years, you can only write off $1,000 of the expense each year, for a three year period.

- *Marketing Expenses*-Estimate the amount of money you will spend to promote your business over the period of the statement. Be sure to include any web site costs as part of the marketing expenses.
- *Insurance*-Include total premiums paid on all of your different business insurance policies.
- *Utilities*-Include costs for heat, light, telephone, garbage removal, water, and so on.
- *Rent*-This includes the amount you pay the landlord or owner of your building.
- *Taxes*-Include all taxes your company will pay: various state and federal payroll taxes, sales taxes, and so on.
- *Interest on loans*-Include the total amount of interest you pay to those from whom you borrow
- *Professional* – Include fees and retainers paid to lawyers, accountants, engineers and so on.
- *Technology costs* – This includes any costs for web site development, new computers or software applications.
- *Miscellaneous costs* – This includes any expenses not covered by one of the above items.

Many times it is easier to split out the expenses as either fixed or variable expenses. Fixed expenses typically do not change over a period of time. Rent in an office building does not change month to month. Whereas materials or inventory may change with the different production or sales levels you may experience. This may be from a seasonal cycle or a response to your advertising campaign.

Managing Expenses

Managing the cash that leaves your company is just as important as regulating the funds that come into it. The first step is to put in to place an effective accounts payable system. You can set one up yourself or get an accountant to do it. There are many software programs available to help with keeping track of accounts payables and accounts receivables in an orderly fashion.

Payroll Costs

The costs of you and your full-time employees are essentially fixed - they remain the same whether business is good or bad, unless you have salespeople working on a commission basis. On the other hand, the salaries of part-time or temporary employees are variable costs from a cash flow standpoint, since they can be adjusted in response to business activity.

Tax Management

Business taxes include income, corporate, unemployment, Social Security (FICA), real estate sales and other categories that vary by locality. By managing your taxes wisely, you may be able to reduce quarterly tax payments when cash is scarce and increase them when business rebounds. To avoid penalties, however, always consult a qualified tax accountant before tinkering your with quarterly payments.

Net Profit

To arrive at the net profit on your income and expense forecast, add your expenses together and subtract that total from the income. Of course, if the expenses exceed the income, you will have a predicted net loss. If this is the case, you will need to reassess your figures and possibly your business idea to see if it really is workable.

Cash Flow Statements

A typical cash flow projection is illustrated in Figure 7.2. Cash flow statements are different than Income and Expense Statements in that you are trying to predict fluctuations in your cash flow, not if you are profitable. It is important when developing your cash flow statement to put the sales receipts and expenses in the category and month that they will be incurred. The cash flow statement will allow you to see when you will have an excess or a shortage of cash. Non-cash items are not included in the cash flow statement, like depreciation.

When creating a cash flow statement you can start with you initial cash investment and the expenses you will incur setting up the business. After that you will include the monthly sales receipts and expenses for the month that they occur. At the bottom of the statement, add together the beginning cash for that period and the sales receipts and subtract the expenses incurred. This will give you your ending cash for that period. If you have to order inventory in one month and pay for it the next month, you may have a shortage of cash for that particular month. This will allow you to draw on a line of credit or other back up funding method if needed.

The techniques we've discussed will not make all your cash flow problems disappear. No matter how well cash is managed, most firms experience periods when funds are tight and a line of credit is needed. However, taking an active role in the management of your company's cash flow ensures that you maximize profits by getting the most benefit from every dollar that comes in to or goes out of your business.

The important thing is to estimate, then go after and get, the money you'll actually need. Shooting for too little money is at least as unwise as asking for too much, and it's not necessarily easier to get lesser amount.

Figure 7.2 Sample Cash Flow Statement

	Starting	Month 1	Month 2		Month 12	Total
Beginning Cash						
Sale Receipts						
Fixed Expenses						
Rent						
Telephone						
Utilities						
Wages						
Variable Expenses						
Purchased Inventory						
Licenses & Permits						
Equipment						
Advertising						
Sales Commissions						
Shipping & Freight						
Auto Expenses						
Travel & Entertainment						
Insurance						
Interest-mortgage						
Interest-loan						
Total Expenses						
Total Cash Flow (Excess or Deficit)						

Chapter 9

50+ Money Sources for Your Business

A key ingredient of business success is knowing how to use other people's money to finance a new or existing business. Obviously, if a company had an unlimited amount of money, there would be no need for outside financing. Executives could lose endless amounts, spend as much as it wanted and not care how long it would take to make the business successful.

TRADITIONAL SOURCES

Sources of money can be divided between the traditional and nontraditional. We will start with a rundown of traditional sources.

Yourself

For the individual businessperson, the most logical place to look for financing is your own assets. These sources include money in bank accounts, certificates of deposit, stocks and bonds, cash value in insurance policies, real estate, home equity, value of hobby collections, automobiles, pension fund, Keogh or IRAs. You don't necessarily need to convert your assets to cash. You could use them as collateral for your loan. For example, your home would be the collateral for a home equity loan. You don't need to sell you home to get the money out of it.

Obviously, if you had sufficient capital, there would be no need to turn to other sources for your needs. But, as noted before, to be successful in a business, most people must know how to use other people's money to finance the new or expanding business.

One word of caution: In today's fast moving economy, most of us have one or more credit cards. It is tempting to take advantage of the availability of money simply by using these cards. Remember, most credit card companies advance money at a much higher rate of interest than you would normally pay a bank or some other financing source. Equally important, although your monthly payments may appear to be small, because of the high interest, your debt compounds and rises quickly.

Family and Relatives

One common source of money is family and relatives. Too often, however, money can get in the way of good family relationships. Therefore, use extreme care in determining whether to approach a family member or relative.

One way you can avoid future problems and disagreements with relatives if they lend you money for your business is to have a written agreement. Spell out clearly the terms to which you and your relatives have agreed:

- Date of the loan
- Loan amount
- Date the loan will be repaid in full
- Dates of loan payments
- Frequently of payments: Monthly, quarterly, etc.
- Amount (percent) of interest
- Collateral, if any
- Signatures by both parties

One important note: It may be wise to make sure the relative from whom you are borrowing has notified his or her spouse. That way, you can ensure that no future problem arises due to any miscommunication.

One other way to work with relatives is to have them co-sign a loan with you. Make sure that everyone clearly understands the loan and co-signing process.

Friends

There is the old adage, "don't mix business with pleasure." Quite frequently, however, friends represent an excellent source of money needed for a small business start-up or an ongoing business. When borrowing from friends, exercise the same caution and documentation as you would from relatives, to make sure that borrowing will not result in the loss of friendship or cause a serious rift to arise.

Your Own Company

If you already have an established company and are in need of money, one of the first places to turn is within the company itself. An established company or business has several options available. These include taking a first or second mortgage on any real estate or property that it owns; borrowing money against machinery or hard assets such as equipment or motor vehicles; or borrowing against a pension fund or inventory that is considered liquid.

Pledging Accounts Receivable   A common method by which companies can obtain a loan is by pledging the firm's accounts receivable in return for a loan. This means that your receivables are pledged or turned over to the bank or loan company that makes the loan. Then, as the receivables are paid, the firm deducts a certain amount of each payment until the loan is paid. Essentially, what the bank or loan company is doing is using your accounts receivable as collateral against the loan.

Factoring   Factoring is another way of using your receivables to raise badly needed cash. In factoring, one goes to a factoring company, which actually buys your accounts receivables.

Assume, for example, that you have $50,000 in accounts receivables and it is a particularly slow time of the year in which you have very little cash flow. The factor will buy your $50,000 in receivables. Possibly they will give you $30,000 or $40,000 for them. The factor then owns the receivables. The amount of discount that the factor takes depends on such things as how old your accounts receivable are, who owes you the money, what you sell, how long you have been in business and so on.

You can find a listing of factors in the Yellow Pages. You can also get a list of such companies from your banker.

Commercial Banks

Banks are the standard lending organizations for business. They represent the largest single source for loans and financing. Their basic business is to provide and manage money for individuals, businesses and organizations. Commercial banks are the main lender for the Small Business Administration.

Interest on loans is commercial bank's main source of income. The amount of interest they charge is based upon two factors: the size and history of the customer and the risk the bank will take in providing the loan.

Interest charges are almost always based upon some factor of the prime interest rate, the lowest rate banks charge their most favored customers. These customers are generally large companies and businesses.

Banks will charge smaller and riskier (in their judgment) customers an interest rate over and above the prime rate. For example, if the customer is a small business with one or two loan experiences, the bank may charge two points over the prime rate. This means is that if the prime rate is eight percent, the small business customer may have to pay ten percent for his or her loan.

Savings and Loan Organizations

These are like banks, but are organized under a different type of charter. Originally established to facilitate the lending of money for home mortgages, they

105

have gradually evolved into full-service banking operations. There are some government restrictions on where and how they can operate as compared to commercial banks. Like banks, their charge for loans is based on the prime rate or some variation of it.

During 1991 and 1992 the Savings and Loan industry was rocked by a great number of scandals involving poor-risk loans. As a result, the remaining saving and loans are taking a very careful look at any business loan application. Many now require any loan be backed up by an equivalent amount of collateral.

Loan Companies

Loan companies, which exist in most U.S. cities and communities, represent one of the largest sources of money in the country. Unlike banks, which obtain from many different sources, loan companies have to rely upon their own capital or raising money, just as other businesses do. Thus their interest rates are usually higher. In some instances, they can be several percentage points above the prime rate.

Loan companies are considered collateral lenders, that is, they rely heavily upon the ability of the borrower's ability to back up every dollar of the loan with a pledge or assignment of some assets. For example, a borrower may have to pledge accounts receivable, put up the mortgage on the company's building, or assign the value of an insurance policy, stocks or bonds.

Loan companies often have different operating policies, and the interest rates they charge may vary as much as five percent from one firm to another. It is therefore prudent to shop around before you settle on a particular loan company. For a listing of loan companies in your area, check the Yellow Pages.

Insurance Companies, Pension Funds and Unions

Existing companies can tap these three sources of money for direct loans or investment purposes. All three are generally interested only in making loans of substantial size, and so would not be interested in making loans to small start-up businesses. Usually their loans are tied to some form of equity ownership. For

106

example, in Minneapolis, the country's largest shopping mall was funded primarily out of a teachers' union pension fund. Here, the pension fund financed the building mortgage. For this, they received a substantial interest in the ownership of the mall.

Credit Unions

A significant source of funding can be found in the credit unions. Credit unions were established with two objectives: to provide a savings vehicle for its members and to be a lender to members in need of loans, primarily for purchasing automobiles and appliances purchases or emergency financial needs. Credit unions are non-profit institutions. Therefore the profits of the credit union go back to the shareholders, which means lower rates for you.

In February of 2003, the Small Business Administration made all credit unions eligible to participate in the SBA loan guarantee program. Since then many credit unions have been actively making small business loans.

In recent years, credit unions have expanded their lending operations to include non-members and investments outside of traditional financial investments. In the past, credit unions would only invest in U. S. Treasury bills and notes, certificates of deposit, and highly rated corporate bonds. Now, they seek out other investments, such as new company start-ups and direct company loans, where they can realize a much higher rate of return or actually secure an equity interest in the company to which they are making the loan.

Micro Enterprise Programs

There are two types of micro enterprise programs: SBA funded microloan programs and private micro enterprise programs. Both private and SBA programs provide very small loans to start-up, newly established, or growing small business concerns. Under the SBA microloan program, the SBA makes funds available to nonprofit community based lenders (intermediaries) which, in turn, make loans to eligible borrowers in amounts up to a maximum of $35,000. The average loan size is about $10,500. Applications are submitted to the local intermediary and all credit decisions are made on the local level.

Each lender has its own lending and credit requirements. However, business owners contemplating application for a microloan should be aware that both programs will generally require some type of collateral, and the personal guarantee of the business owner. The SBA program also requires its intermediaries to provide business based training and technical assistance to its borrowers.

Small Business Investment Companies

These are privately owned companies licensed and insured by the U.S. Small Business Administration to provide capital to small firms. Small Business Investment Companies usually focus on specific industries such as medically-oriented high technology enterprises, or agricultural, manufacturing or real estate companies.

Several Small Business Investment Companies exist in each state; to find them, contact the nearest Office of Small Business Administration or obtain a listing of them for your area from the U.S. Department of Commerce or your local Congressional representative. They are also available on the Internet at www.sba.gov.

Small Business Innovation Research Fund

The SBIR program is funded by 11 federal agencies that publish a list of specific program needs, problems or opportunities. The agencies invest small amounts of money in the concept and feasibility stages of development. The second phase is developing a prototype. In the final phase of moving the product to the commercial market is handled by non-SBIR funding sources. More information on this program can be found at **www.sba.gov**. Some examples of federal agencies that participate in this program are:

- Department of Defense
- Department of Health & Human Services
- NASA
- Department of Energy
- National Science Foundation
- Department of Agriculture
- Department of Transportation
- Department of Education

Certified Development Companies

The SBA 504 Certified Development Company (CDC) Program provides growing businesses with long-term, fixed-rate financing for major fixed assets, such as land and buildings. A Certified Development Company is a nonprofit corporation set up to contribute to the economic development of its community. CDCs work with the SBA and private-sector lenders to provide financing to small businesses. There are about 270 CDCs nationwide. Each CDC covers a specific geographic area. The funds in this program are used for:

Business district revitalization

Expansion of exports

Expansion of minority business development

Rural development

Enhanced economic competition

Restructuring because of federally mandated standards or policies

Changes necessitated by federal budget cutbacks

Expansion of small business concerns owned and controlled by veterans

Expansion of small business concerns owned and controlled by women

To locate a CDC in your area, go to: www.sba.gov and search certified development company.

Government Assistance Programs

Some government program, because they are supported by public funds, are aimed at solving a particular problem. Most programs are either loans, grants, contract awards, or credits. Contract awards are for specific products that the government uses and credits are generally tax incentives to companies for providing new jobs or economic growth for a specific area. The following are some organizations to contact for more information:

- Local Economic Development Associations
- Local Enterprise Zones
- State Office of Economic Development (may have different name in different states)
- State Business Development Fund (may be called Finance Authority, Industrial Revenue Bond Funds, Board of Investments)
- State Procurement Technical Assistance Centers

Import and Export Financing

If your company is doing business globally, you probably need help with import and export financing. There are a few different places that offer financing for this type of activity.

The SBA has an International Trade Loan and an Export Working Capital Loan Programs. To learn more go to the SBA web site at **www.sba.gov** or check out the SBA chapter in this book.

The Export-Import Bank also has a variety of programs to help small businesses export more products overseas. The first is a short term insurance program that allows the small business to offer credit terms to the foreign customer. This is important because many foreign buyers expect the United States business to offer this service. This program protects the exporter from payment default of the foreign customer. The second program is a Medium Term Export Credit Insurance. This program allows the exporter to offer credit terms of 1-7 years to the foreign customer. The Ex-Im Bank will insure against default of the foreign customer in case of commercial or political risk. The third program is a Working Capital Guarantee program that allows commercial lenders to make working capital loans to U. S. exporters for export-related expenses by substantially reducing the risks associated with these loans.

110

Private Investors / Angels

These individuals or groups make investments and loans, usually in exchange for an equity interest in a company. They work with existing concerns and new business start-ups. The objective of and the size of funds available from private investors vary widely. Some, for example, confine their activities to high technology firms, while others, may invest or lend money to retailers.

Generally speaking, private investors only want to make an investment in the company. Some limit their participation to under $50,000; others may consider only companies in need of a half million dollars or more. Most can be found through local bankers, accountants or lawyers or your local newspaper's Sunday classified advertising pages.

ACE-Net, now known as Active Capital was started by the Small Business Administration, but as of April 2000, the organization has become an independent not-for-profit. ACE-Net provides private investors and entrepreneurs a way of finding each other through an Internet database. Currently the 358 active investors and 328 entrepreneur company listings. ACE-Net is for companies that are not sole-proprietorships, partnerships, development stage companies or investment companies. To find out more about Active Capital go to: www.activecapital.com.

In addition, more private investors/angels can be found by searching the Angel Capital Associations website at www.angelcapitalassociation.org.

Venture Capitalists

A form of private investor is the venture capitalist. This individual or group almost always provides funding for an equity or ownership interest in the firm. The venture capitalist is usually interested in high-technology, high growth or technology-related new business start-ups. Thus, they are concerned primarily with companies that are developing a new product and that usually will not have access to traditional money sources.

Ventures capitalists are like private investors in that they generally will not take an active role in the management or everyday affairs of the company they are

111

providing funds. Their role can be passive, although they will typically require that they join the company's board of directors. Some venture capital companies have changed over the past few years. Many are bringing more to companies than they have in the past. Some venture capitalists will help high growth companies find experienced high level managers or contacts to potential customers. Most venture capitalists are looking for a minimum of 30% return on their money and a very clear exit strategy for the company within 5 years.

New Markets Venture Capital Companies (NMVCC) are regulated and overseen by the SBA to make sure the public policy objectives are being met. The NMVCC is eligible for grant and operational assistance from the SBA. At least 80% of the NMVCCs investments must be in smaller enterprises by SBA guidelines, in low-income geographic areas as defined by the SBA and must have equity capital investments, including common stock, preferred stock or some subordinated debt structures.

Leasing Companies

The role of leasing companies and organizations has traditionally been tied to providing motor vehicles for individuals and companies. Gradually this role has changed. Leasing companies began moving into fleet leasing, consisting of up to hundreds of automobiles, trucks, cargo carriers, buses, and airplanes. Many have even taken over the financing of cargo and passenger vessels.

In recent years, these same leasing companies have further diversified their operations; they are now known to pay for the purchase of new inventory and provide money for leasehold improvements such as decorating and remodeling. They may even provide money for working capital. Since leasing companies derive their income from the use of capital, many have recently moved into many areas previously considered the domain of banks and loan companies.

Leasing is used mainly for heavy equipment purchases, but now is being used more and more for telephone equipment and computer purchases.

Government Grants

The SBA does not have grants available for individuals who want to start, operate or expand a small business. Although the infomercials are misleading, the federal government does not have grant money available for small businesses. Grants must be approved by Congress and included as part of annual federal budget. As of the writing of this book, the state of the federal budget and most state's budgets are in the process of being cut. Most of the grant funds available are for other government organizations or not-for-profit programs. If you would like to check out grants that are available, you can do a search of program at the Catalog of Federal Domestic Assistance web site at www.cfda.gov.

There are some grant programs available to small businesses including the Small Business Innovation Research program (discussed earlier). But most of these grants are for developing new technologies.

The best place to look for grant money is through organizations that either have contests or cash prizes. One example may be a business plan competition offered by a local financial institution or magazine with cash awards.

In looking for grants, it never hurts to call your local city hall, county offices, or state department of economic development to see if they have any new programs for their area. Some government organizations may be trying to increase specific types of businesses, like women-owned or manufacturing businesses in their community.

NONTRADITIONAL SOURCES

Non-traditional sources are unlimited in number and type, but you need to be creative to acquire the necessary funding from them for your start-up or expanding business.

Customers

Customers or potential customers can be an excellent source of funding. Consider the following examples: Two engineers worked together at the same company. On their own time, they develop a new plastic, the manufacturing of which requires a large capital investment. When used as raw material, their plastic, is one-third the cost of the product companies or customers are currently using. The engineers contact a large potential user, who realizes that the new plastic can reduce her raw material costs significantly. Subsequently, she lends the two engineers the money necessary to start their own business. In return for her investment, the user receives a contract assuring her company of getting 75 percent of the manufacturing output of the new plastic.

Another example is that of a cosmetologist who wants to open her own salon. In conversations with a customer, it turns out that the customer likewise wants to have her own business. The customer invests in the salon and the two form a partnership. The cosmetologist manages the salon and the other employees; her partner participated in the day-to-day affairs of the salon handling bookkeeping, advertising and customer service.

Suppliers

Suppliers can be a great source of funding because they can often be assured of becoming the principal supplier to a customer they=ve helped; this holds true especially in highly competitive fields.

Suppliers will often provide supplemental equipment that is necessary for use with the products they provide. For example, food wholesalers will often provide display cases, shelving and other equipment.

For example, let's say a bakery-delicatessen in a major city decided it was necessary to open a second location to accommodate customers who had moved to another, growing residential area. To finance the expansion, the owners contact their major suppliers. A milling company advances them $100,000 at an interest rate substantially below prevailing market rates to purchase ovens. For this consideration, the bakery owners promise to buy from the supplier a minimum of 75

114

percent of their flour for the next three years. The owners also obtain funds from their deli meat supplier to purchase to purchase their new refrigeration deli display cases.

Employees

Typically raising money from employees happens in Employee Stock Option Plans in larger companies. But raising money from employees has become more common lately when an owner wants to sell their portion of the business. Instead of an outsider coming in to run the business, management can do a buy-out or the employees can try to raise funds by themselves to keep the business. If you are a small company, this may not be an alternative for raising cash. Sometimes when you allow employees to become partners, they think they can create more of the vision for the company going forward. There may be more problems with employees not all agreeing with your plans or ideas.

Bartering

Bartering is the act of trading products or services with another company or individual. Bartering allows you to receive products or services that you need for your business in addition to conserving your cash. In using this method of financing, look for businesses where you can benefit from each other's customer base or product or service offerings. For example, an advertising firm could produce a small radio campaign for a computer company in exchange for a new computer for the advertising company. One thing to remember when bartering is that the transaction is viewed as income by the IRS.

One way to manage your bartering activities is to join Itex. Itex is the largest bartering system in the country processing over $250 million transactions per year. Itex allows you to take "Itex dollars" as payment, increasing your sales and allows you to spend you dollars at over 11,000 businesses. To find out more, go to: www.itexmn.com.

Joint Ventures

Joint ventures are partnerships where each party is an active part of the transaction. Joint ventures can help to keep costs down for each company by sharing the work load and splitting the expenses. For example, two financial planners or accountants can share office space and a receptionist to help control costs. This type of sharing of expenses is very common in beauty salons. Typically in a salon, the hair stylist "rents" a chair and pays a portion of the receptionist, utilities and marketing expenses of the salon.

Joint ventures are a great way to start a business. If you have a product, but no customers, you can find a partner that has a list of customers that may be interested in your products. If you have a list of customers but no product, it is easy to find products with the help of the internet. Look at the success of Ebay. Ebay has a list of customers, all you have to do is find the products that meet their needs and wants.

Joint ventures take very little cash to start. Profits can be split by the partners, so everyone wins. Joint ventures can be small agreements or larger agreements for complex research and development efforts. Joint ventures are really only limited to a business owner's creativity and negotiation skills.

Local Development Companies

These organizations have been formed to attract new business to particular areas. They are frequently established in rural communities and small towns. Usually they are made up of local banks, real estate firms and local business association members who band together to bring in new industry. These nonprofit institutions are in a position to offer land and buildings, even capital. Local development companies often obtain their funds from unusual sources; for example, one in Minnesota is funded through a local board of education.

Franchising

Offering your business concept as a franchise to other entrepreneurs is one way of expanding your business and raising some additional financing. Franchising is not a start-up funding source, but one that can be used in expansion or growth. Franchising allows you to profit from sharing your secrets to success with others. To be successful at franchising your business concept, you need to identify and understand exactly what processes make you successful and how can you train someone else on these procedures. The paperwork to set up a franchise for your business concept can be complex. To learn more about franchising, contact the International Franchise Association.

Licensing

Licensing is like franchising except you are selling the rights for someone to duplicate a technology process or service system for a fee. Licensing is easier to set up than franchising. Since licensing is specific to a certain technology or process, the number of potential buyers of the license may be more limited than franchising. In the past many third world countries purchase licenses for technological advances that would take too long and too much money to develop on their own. Licensing is the transfer of specific knowledge for a stated amount of time. It is very important to be clear about the technology or process that you are selling. To learn more contact experts in your field to help you identify possible processes that may be licensable.

Business Incubators

From the National Business Incubation Association: "Incubators nurture young firms, helping them to survive and grow during the start-up period when they are most vulnerable. Incubators provide hands-on management assistance, access to financing and orchestrated exposure to critical business or technical support services. They also offer entrepreneurial firms shared office services, access to equipment, flexible leases and expandable space — all under one roof. An incubation program's main goal is to produce successful graduates — businesses

117

that are financially viable and freestanding when they leave the incubator, usually in two to three years."

Incubators are much like venture capitalists in that some are specific to an industry while others concentrate on a mix of businesses. Businesses that are in incubators today are generally ones with new or innovative technologies.

To find an incubator in your area, go to the National Business Incubation web site at www.nbia.org.

Cash Advances for Visa and MasterCard Receipts

Typically to be eligible your business needs to be processing over $5,000 in Visa or MasterCard receipts per month. Lenders will take a portion of the on going credit card receipts as a form of payment on the loan. Normally there are no up front costs, fixed payments or fixed time frame for repayment.

Purchase Order Financing

Purchase order financing is used in cases where your suppliers want to be paid up front and your customers want to pay you in 30-60 days. There is no cash flow during manufacturing, delivery or until invoices are paid. The funding source will pay your supplier directly reserving your own cash to pay your other business expenses.

Advertising for Money

You can actively seek funding by running a display advertisement in the business section or under the appropriate heading in the classified ads of your local newspaper. Specify the amount of money needed and the type of business for which it will be used. Confidentiality for both parties can be maintained through the use of a post office box or newspaper box number.

An example of an advertisement recently placed in the business opportunity section of a newspaper's classified advertising pages is shown in Figure 8.1. In this ad, the party seeking the loan was interested in finding someone who would make a straight $50,000 loan. Another alternative could have offered an opportunity to buy into the business, as shown in the sample ad in Figure 8.2.

Figure 8-1

Business Investment

Opportunity

Rapidly growing retail store seeks additional

capital of up to $50,000 for expansion purposes.

Low risk investment with 10% interest return on

your investments. For information write P.O. Box

27612, Minneapolis, MN 55426 or call 612-957-3344.

Figure 8-2

Business Investment

Opportunity

Rapidly growing retail store seeks financial

partner interested in investing up to $50,000

in exchange for an equity ownership in the store.

For additional information write P.O. Box 27612

Minneapolis, MN 55426 or call 612-957-3344

Another alternative for money for small businesses is that which is provided by the U. S. Small Business Administration, which will be discussed in the next chapter.

Cash Flow Financing Sources

The trick to managing cash flow is to get the money to come in faster while paying it out as slow as possible. The following are some ways to increase the cash coming into your business.

Deposits – Asking your customers for deposits is a common practice in event ticket sales, infomercials and many other businesses. Think about ways you could ask for payment up front. For example, when Mark Victor Hansen and Jack Canfield created the book, "Chicken Soup For The Soul", they could not get a publisher to produce the book. So both Jack and Mark went to their friends and family and started making a list of people who would buy the book if it was available. They took the list to the publishers again and this time a small publisher decided to promote the book. Jack and Mark could have taken it one step further and started asking for payment on the books with a specified delivery date. Then they could have printed up the number of books for which they had received orders. How can you add initial deposits, down payments or prepayments as an option of payment for your customers? If customers will not pay deposits, can you give them an incentive to do so? Maybe 10% off their order for prepayment?

If you are opening a restaurant, could you offer 1 year of meals (1 per month) for a discounted price? People could give you money now for services to be rendered in the future. The possibilities are endless.

Memberships - We have seen an increase in membership opportunities in the past 10 years. Look at the success of Costco and Sam's Club Warehouses. Customers actually PAY to be able to spend money at these stores. Seems odd, but can you create a club where members would pay a monthly or annual fee to be able to get discounts on your products or services? Brainstorm ideas with business associates to come up with some new ideas. Dan Kennedy has used this method very successfully by developing Silver, Gold, Gold + and Platinum groups. Each group has special benefits at increasing prices.

Chapter 10

Small Business Administration Programs

The Small Business Administration (SBA) was created in 1953 through Congress's passage of the Small Business Act. It was established to help create and maintain successful small businesses by offering financing, training, assistance and advocacy programs for small business.

The Small Business Administration programs have assisted many individuals starting and forming new businesses, as well as owners of existing small businesses. The SBA provides assistance in a wide variety of areas: finance, marketing, production, human resource management, loans, export, government procurement, innovation and research, women's business ownership, minority business ownership, education, and training. It is also the government's principal arm for disaster assistance and maintains four Disaster Assistance offices.

Headquartered in Washington, D.C., the SBA has ten regional offices and approximately 100 district, branch and post-of-duty offices in all 50 states, the District of Columbia, Guam, Puerto Rico and the Virgin Islands. The head of the SBA is appointed by the President and confirmed by the Senate.

The SBA has a number of major partners in providing assistance. These include: SCORE, Small Business Development Centers (SBDC), Small Business Institutes (SBI), and Business Information Centers (BIC)

SCORE Association

SCORE is made up of executives from both small and large businesses, who volunteer their time to provide free counseling to small business and individuals interested in starting small businesses. They also conduct regular seminars and workshops on various topics. SCORE has 390 chapters and 270 satellite offices across the country. They can be found by going to the SBA website at www.sba.gov.

Small Business Development Centers

SBDCs are a cooperative effort of local, state and federal governments. The bulk of the funding comes from the SBA. There are approximately 900 SBDCs and sub-centers throughout the country. Almost all of them are affiliated with colleges, universities, or vocational technical training schools or other educational institutions. SBDCs provide a wide range of assistance to new business start-ups and operating small businesses. They offer assistance in counseling, market studies, business plan writing, advertising and public relations, and financial analysis. In

122

addition, they offer courses on setting up and operating small businesses.

THE SBA GUARANTEED LOAN PROGRAM

The SBA is best known for its activities in the field of lending and providing financial assistance to small businesses. Clouding these activities is a common misconception that the SBA is like a bank, lending money directly to individuals and businesses. Nothing could be further from the truth.

The SBA does, however, provide a wide range of lending and financial assistance activities. We'll discuss many of these functions. For detailed information on each of them, you should contact your nearest SBA office or their web site at www.sba.gov.

The SBA offers several categories of loans, most which fall under the SBA Guaranteed Loan Program. There are a number of reasons why a company or individual turns to the SBA:

- The small business owner needs more time than a traditional bank will allow to pay back a loan.
- The borrower lacks sufficient collateral
- The borrower is the owner of a start-up company, and lacks the business experience required by most banks.

SBA loans are available to existing and start-up companies alike. There are no restrictions as to the number of SBA loans a company or individual may have, as long as the SBA's exposure does not exceed $750,000. For example, a company can have three different SBA loans, all from different banks or lending agencies, provided the total amount of the loans is not greater than $750,000.

Under the Small Business Act, all loans made under the various SBA loan programs must be of "sound value or so secured as to reasonably ensure repayment." This means that the individual or company asking for the loan must demonstrate good business judgment, have made some equity investment in the

123

company, and have some collateral to back up the loan.

With regard to providing SBA loans, the agency is interested in encouraging new business start-ups and providing for the continuation in business of small businesses in need of financing.

Qualifying for an SBA Loan

To qualify for a SBA loan, a business must show that it is a small business that is independently owned and not part of some other large company or organization. It cannot be a major or the dominant firm in the industry. And most important, the small business must show that has the ability to repay the loan.

Collateral Requirements Like all lending agencies, the SBA generally attempts to secure its loans with as much collateral as possible. Collateral is defined by Webster as "designating of security given as a pledge for the fulfillment of an obligation; hence secured or guaranteed by property." This can include a wide variety of items such as accounts receivable, stocks, bonds, cash value in life insurance, equipment, fixtures, raw materials, inventory, automobiles, trucks, furniture or real estate. Many lenders will also put a lien on your house as collateral for a loan and have you personally guarantee the amount of the loan. Frequently, the collateral put up for the loan is exactly what the loan is used for. For example, to purchase machinery or add inventory the machinery or inventory becomes the collateral.

This does not mean that, for every dollar that they guarantee in a loan, the SBA requires that a dollar of collateral be made available to them. It does mean that the individual or company making a loan application must make every reasonable effort to secure the loan with as much collateral as possible.

Equity Requirements The SBA also requires that loan applicants have a sufficient amount of his or her own equity in the business. In other words, the party seeking

124

the loan, must at one point have invested a reasonable amount of their own personal money in the business. Although there is no clear definition of what the amount of equity is, it is expected that applicants will invest a fair amount of their own capital if starting a new business, or if it is an ongoing business, that they would have made an earlier investment of their own money or assets.

What is a Small Business?

In order to qualify for an SBA loan, an existing business must be qualified as "small" under the SBA size and standard guidelines. The standards differ by industry and may be measured in terms of dollars or number of employees.

These standards are described below:

- *Wholesale*. The average number of employees per pay period for the preceding 12 months may not exceed 100 (this includes part-time and temporary employees).
- *Retail*. The average annual receipts for the last three years must be less than $6.5 million. A few, such as grocery stores, department stores, car dealerships and appliance dealerships have higher limits.
- *Service Company*. The average annual receipts for the last three years must be less than $6.5 million.
- *Construction*. The average annual receipts for the last three years must be less than $31 million, except for certain dredging and cleanup activities. Special trade construction operations, that is, operations that work in a special construction vocational activity, are limited to the last three years' sales average of not more than $13 million.

The preceding standards are not, however, cast in concrete. Certain types of businesses may exceed these limits, yet be accepted for a loan. If you do not meet the criteria for your specific industry, contact your nearest SBA office to determine whether a variance will be accepted.

125

For types of firms that are excluded from participating in the SBA loan program, contact you local SBA office. Also, individuals who are currently in prison, on probation or on parole for a serious offense may not make apply for a loan.

Applying for a Guaranteed Loan

The SBA has regular procedures for applying for loans, and these usually take anywhere from a day or two up to a couple of months depending on the complexity of the deal. To apply for an SBA guaranteed loan, the small business borrower must go through several steps and complete a number of SBA forms and applications. To complete these forms, the borrower needs to have all of the information found in the checklist shown in figure 9.1, and must complete the forms listed in Appendix A.

Once approved, the loan is made through a bank or an authorized banking agency. Although the loan is actually supplied by the bank, the SBA operates as an insurance company for the loan; in the event that the borrower defaults on the loan, the SBA will guarantee the payment of up to 80 percent of the outstanding balance of the loan.

Loans under the Guaranteed Loan Program are made in conjunction with three parties: the SBA, the small business borrowing the funds and the private lender. In most cases the private lender is a bank. The flow chart in Figure 9.2 shows the SBA guaranteed loan application process.

Figure 9.2

> 1. The Small Business seeking the loan submits its loan application to the bank or lending agency.
>
> 2. Lending agency forwards loan application to the SBA, together with its credit analysis.
>
> 3. SBA approves of the loan application.
>
> 4. Lending agency closes or concurs with the loan.
>
> 5. Lender and borrower agree on a repayment program.
>
> 6. Small Business borrower receives funds from the lender.
>
> 7. Small Business borrower begins making repayment of the loan with interest.

Interest Rates Two rate structures are available for SBA guaranteed loans: fixed and variable. Variable rate loans can be adjusted monthly, quarterly, semiannually or annually and float with the prime rate. Fixed-rate loans do not change during the life of the loan. The maximum allowable rate for both types of loans is 2-3/4 percent over the prime rate for loans of seven years and longer, and 2-1/4 percent over the prime rate for loans up to seven years. The prime rate is the minimum New York prime rate as published in the Wall Street Journal.

Maturity The length of a loan is determined by the use of the loan proceeds. Working capital loans are generally limited to seven years. Loans for machinery and capital equipment are based on the life of the equipment but not generally over ten years. Real estate loans have a maximum maturity of 25 years.

Uses of Loan Proceeds SBA loans can be used by existing or start-up businesses and can be used for the purchase of an existing business. This means that the individual or company taking out a SBA loan can use the proceeds for working capital, to purchase inventory, plant and equipment, raw material, goods in process, finished goods, adding labor, making payments for accounts payable and for almost any expense or asset need of the enterprise.

Repayment Terms

Once an SBA loan application is made and approved, representatives of the business meet with their bank lending officer to discuss various repayment points. These include repayment terms of the loan, commencement date for repayment, length of the loan period and schedule for repayment.

These points are determined by each particular business. Factors taken into consideration include projected sales and earnings, use of the loan proceeds, business equity, management and an analysis of the small business and its operation. Indeed, the SBA and the bank, or lending agency are not interested in setting a repayment program that will impair the stability of the business and place the proceeds of the loan and the business in jeopardy.

The SBA forms required for any loan are shown in Figure 9.3.

Checklist 9.3 Small Business Administration Loan Forms

1. Application for Loan: SBA form 4, 4I
2. Statement of Personal History: SBA form 912
3. Personal Financial Statement: SBA form 413
4. Detailed, signed Balance Sheet and Profit & Loss Statements current (within 90 days of application) and last three (3) fiscal years Supplementary Schedules required on Current Financial Statements.
5. Detailed one (1) year projection of Income & Finances (please attach written explanation as to how you expect to achieve same).
6. A list of names and addresses of any subsidiaries and affiliates, including concerns in which the applicant holds a controlling (but not necessarily a majority) interest and other concerns that may be affiliated by stock ownership, franchise, proposed merger or otherwise with the applicant.

128

7. Certificate of Doing Business (If a corporation, stamp corporate seal on SBA form 4 section 12).

8. By Law, the Agency may not guarantee a loan if a business can obtain funds on reasonable terms from a bank or other private source. A borrower therefore must first seek private financing.

   A company must be independently owned and operated, not dominant in its field and must meet certain standards of size in terms of employees or annual receipts. Loans cannot b made to speculative businesses, newspapers, or businesses engaged in gambling.

   Applicants for loans must also agree to comply with SBA regulation that there will be no discrimination in employment or services to the public, based on race, color, religion, national origin, sex or marital status.

9. Signed Business Federal Income Tax Returns for previous three (3) year.

10. Signed Personal Federal Income Tax Returns of principals for previous three (3) years.

11. Personal Resume including business experience of each principal.

12. Brief history of the business and its problems: Include an explanation of why the SBA loan is needed and how it will help the business.

13. Copy of Business Lease (or note from landlord giving terms of proposed lease.

14. For purchase of an existing business:
    a. Current Balance Sheet and Profit & Loss Statement of business to be purchased.
    b. Previous two (2) years Federal Income Tax Returns of the business.
    c. Propose Bill of Sale Including: Terms of Sale.
    d. Asking Price with schedule of:
       1. Inventory
       2. Machinery & Equipment
       3. Furniture & Fixtures

Copies of each of these forms is found on the SBA web site at www.sba.gov Search on Loan Forms.

One important element that is not provided for in any formal format or form that generally must be submitted when applying for an SBA loan is a Business Plan.

129

SPECIALIZED GUARANTEED SBA LOAN PROGRAMS

Pollution Control Loans

These types of loans are offered through the guaranteed loan program. They must meet the same credit criteria and conditions as the regular guaranteed loans. The maximum amount is $1 million, or up to 85 percent of the needed amount of money. Proceeds must be used to finance the planning, design or installation of a pollution control facility which is defined as real or personal property that is likely to help prevent, reduce, abate or control noise, air or water pollution.

International Trade Loans

Also offered through the guaranteed loan program, these loans to help small businesses finance their export or overseas business. A firm can seek funds through this program if, for example, it needs working capital to purchase equipment or to finance facility expansion in order to take care of their overseas sales. The program also helps firms buying or selling products overseas. Frequently, payment by the overseas buyer is made by a letter of credit, which tells the supplier that they are guaranteed payment, since the money has been deposited in a bank.

This letter of credit cannot, however, be turned into cash by the small business until shipment is actually made of whatever has been ordered. It may take up to several months for a small business to produce the order; thus, working capital is needed to finance the business during this timeframe. This is where the International Trade Loan comes into play. These loans are limited to a maximum of $1 million or up to 85 percent of the needed funds, to a maximum of $250,000 for working capital.

International Trade Loan Eligibility

If your business is preparing to engage in or is already engaged in international trade, or is adversely affected by competition from imports, the International Trade Loan Program is designed for you.

The applicant must establish that the loan will significantly expand or develop an export market, is currently adversely affected by import competition, will upgrade equipment or facilities to improve competitive position, or must be able to provide a business plan that reasonably projects export sales sufficient to cover the loan.

Use Of Loan Proceeds

The proceeds of a SBA International Trade loan may be used to acquire, construct, renovate, modernize, improve or expand facilities and equipment to be used in the United States to produce goods or services involved in international trade; or the refinancing of existing indebtedness that is not structured with reasonable terms and conditions. There can be no working capital as part of an IT loan or as part of any refinancing.

A small business concern is engaged in international trade if, as determined by SBA, "the small business concern is in a position to expand existing export markets or develop new export markets."

A small business concern is adversely affected by international trade if, as determined by SBA, "the small business concern (i) is confronting increased competition with foreign firms in the relevant market; and (ii) is injured by such competition."

International Trade Loan Maturities

Loans for facilities or equipment can have maturities of up to 25 years.

Interest Rates

Fees

International Trade Loan Maximum Loan Amount

131

The maximum gross amount ($2 million) and SBA-guaranteed amount ($1.5 million) for an IT loan is the same as a regular 7(a) loan. However, there is an exception to the maximum SBA 7(a) guaranty amount to one borrower (including affiliates).

The maximum guaranteed amount can go up to $1,750,000 under the following circumstances: (1) The small business has been approved for an IT loan, and (2) the business has applied for a separate working capital loan (or loans) under EWCP and/or other 7(a) loan programs. When there is an IT loan and a separate working capital loan, the maximum SBA guaranty on the combined loans can be up to $1,750,000 as long as the SBA guaranty on the working capital loan does not exceed $1,250,000. In all cases, to receive the maximum SBA guaranty amount of $1,750,000, the financing package for the small business must include an IT loan that was approved after December 7, 2004.

International Trade Loan Guaranty Percent

For the International trade Loan, SBA can guaranty up to 85 percent of loans of $150,000 and less, and up to 75 percent of loans above $150,000. The maximum guaranteed amount is $1,250,000.

Loan Program Collateral

Only collateral located in the United States, its territories and possessions is acceptable as collateral under this program. The lender must take a first lien position (or first mortgage) on items financed under an international trade loan. Additional collateral may be required, including personal guarantees, subordinate liens, or items that are not financed by the loan proceeds.

OTHER SBA LOAN PROGRAMS

In addition to the previously discussed guaranteed loans, the SBA offers a number of other specific loan programs, which fall into several different categories:

- SBA short term loans
- Seasonal line of credit
- Small general contractor
- Export revolving line
- Handicapped assistance
- Veterans and disabled veterans
- Development company loan program
- Micro loan program

SBA Short-Term Loans

CAPLines is the umbrella program under which the SBA helps small businesses meet their short-term and cyclical working-capital needs. A CAPLines loan, Except the Small Asset-Based Line, can be for any dollar amount that does not exceed SBA's limit. (See the 7(a) Loan program for more information on SBA's Basic Requirements.)

There are five short-term working-capital loan programs for small businesses under the CAPLines umbrella:

Seasonal Line: These are advances against anticipated inventory and accounts receivable help during peak seasons when businesses experience seasonal sales fluctuations. Can be revolving or non-revolving.

Contract Line: Finances the direct labor and material cost associated with performing assignable contract(s). Can be revolving or non-revolving.

Builders Line: If you are a small general contractor or builder constructing or renovating commercial or residential buildings, this can finance direct labor-and material costs. The building project serves as the collateral, and loans can be revolving or non-revolving.

Standard Asset-Based Line: This is an asset-based revolving line of credit for businesses unable to meet credit standards associated with long-term credit. It provides financing for cyclical growth, recurring and/or short-term needs. Repayment comes from converting short-term assets into cash, which is remitted to the lender. Businesses continually draw from this line of credit, based on existing assets, and repay as their cash cycle dictates. This line generally is used by businesses that provide credit to other businesses. Because these loans require continual servicing and monitoring of collateral, additional fees may be charged by the lender.

Small Asset-Based Line: This is an asset-based revolving line of credit of up to $200,000.

133

It operates like a standard asset-based line except that some of the stricter servicing requirements are waived, providing the business can consistently show repayment ability from cash flow for the full amount.

Maximum Loan Amounts

Except the Small Asset-Based Line, CAPLine loans follow SBA's <u>maximum loan amounts</u>. The Small Asset-Based Line has a maximum loan amount of $200,000.

Eligibility

Although most small businesses are eligible for SBA loans, some types of businesses are ineligible and a case-by-case determination must be made by the Agency. Eligibility is generally determined by four factors:

Type Of Businesses Eligible
Size
Use Of Proceeds

Loan Maturities

Each of the five lines of credit has a maturity of up to five (5) years,but, because each is tailored to an individual business's needs, a shorter initial maturity may be established. CAPLines funds can be used as needed throughout the term of the loan to purchase assets, as long as sufficient time is allowed to convert the assets into cash at maturity.

<u>Interest Rates</u>
<u>Fees</u>
<u>Guaranty Percent</u>

Collateral

Holders of at least 20% ownership in the business are generally required to guaranty the loan. Although inadequate collateral will not be the sole reason for denial of a loan request, the nature and value of that collateral does factor into the credit decision.

Contract Loan Program The contract loan program provides working capital to those companies in need of money to meet, complete and fulfill the obligations of a short term contract. To qualify, a business must have been in operation for 12 months or more preceding the date of application. The loan amount is limited to the cash requirement for the labor and material portion of the contract only.

For example, a clothing manufacturer may have received a contract to produce 25,000 pair of pants. The contract is between the small business textile manufacturer and a leading nationwide discount store chain. To complete the contract, the producer needs to purchase the cloth material from which the pants will be made. Having exhausted his or her alternatives for raising the necessary capital to purchase the raw material, the producer can apply for such a loan from the SBA. Each loan of this nature applies to a specific contract that the borrower has.

Seasonal Line of Credit

The seasonal line of credit is used to finance working capital needs arising from the seasonal upswings of a business. Typical uses are to build up inventory and pay for increased labor costs resulting from seasonal trends. The SBA will guarantee as much as 85 percent of the loan up to $750,000. For loans of up to $155,000, the agency can guarantee up to 90 percent of the principal. Finally, the term of the seasonal line of credit loan cannot be more then 12 months from the date of the SBA's first disbursement.

These loans are available under the guaranty loan program and must meet the same criteria as other SBA guaranteed loans.

Small General Contractor Loans

The Small General Contractor Loan is a short-term program designed to finance residential and commercial construction or rehabilitation for resale. The applicant must be a construction contractor; a company that subcontracts all work is not eligible. The SBA can guarantee as much as 85 percent of the loan up to $750,000. The maximum guaranty for loans up to $155,000 is 90 percent.

The loan maturity cannot be more than 36 months plus a reasonable estimate of the time it takes to complete the construction or renovation. Principal repayment may be required in a single payment when the project is sold.

For such loans, three documents are required:

1. A letter from the mortgage lender doing business in the area, affirming that permanent mortgage financing for qualified purchasers of comparable real

estate is normally available in the project's area.

2. A letter from an independently licensed real estate broker with three years' experience on the project area. The letter must state whether a market for the proposed structure exists and whether it is compatible with other buildings in the neighborhood.

3. A letter from an independent architect, appraiser or engineer, confirming availability of the construction inspection and certification at intervals during the project.

Export Revolving Line

The Export Working Capital Program (EWCP) was designed to provide short-term working capital to exporters.

The SBA's Export Working Capital Program (EWCP) supports export financing to small businesses when that financing is not otherwise available on reasonable terms. The program encourages lenders to offer export working capital loans by guaranteeing repayment of up to $1.5 million or 90 percent of a loan amount, whichever is less. A loan can support a single transaction or multiple sales on a revolving basis.

Designed to provide short-term working capital to exporters, the EWCP is a combined effort of the SBA and the Export-Import Bank. The two agencies have joined their working capital programs to offer a unified approach to the government's support of export financing. The EWCP uses a one-page application form and streamlined documentation with turnaround usually 10 days or less. A letter of prequalification is also available from the SBA.
Maximum 7(a) Loan Amounts

Export Working Capital Program Eligibility (EWCP)
In addition to the eligibility standards listed below, an applicant must be in business for a full year (not necessarily in exporting) at the time of application. SBA may waive this requirement if the applicant has sufficient export trade experience. Export management companies or export-trading companies my use this program; however, title must be taken in the goods being exported to be eligible.

Most small businesses are eligible for SBA loans; some types of businesses are ineligible and a case-by-case determination must be made by the Agency. Eligibility is generally determined Business Type, Use of Proceeds, Size of Business, and Availability of Funds from other sources. The following links provide more detailed information about each of these areas.

The proceeds of an EWCP loan must be used to finance the working capital needs associated with a single or multiple transactions of the exporter.

Proceeds may not be used to finance professional export marketing advice or services, foreign business travel, participating in trade shows or U.S. support staff in overseas, except to the extent it relates directly to the transaction being financed. In addition, "proceeds may not be used" to make payments to owners, to pay delinquent withholding taxes, or to pay existing debt.

The applicant must establish that the loan will significantly expand or develop an export market, is currently adversely affected by import competition, will upgrade equipment or facilities to improve competitive position, or must be able to provide a business plan that reasonably projects export sales sufficient to cover the loan.

Export Working Capital Program (EWCP) Maturities
SBA guarantees the short-term working capital loans made by participating Lenders to exporters. An export loan can be for a single or multiple transactions. If the loan is for a single transaction, the maturity should correspond to the length of the transaction cycle with a maximum maturity of 18 months. If the loan is for a revolving line of credit, the maturity is typically twelve (12) months, with annual reissuances allowed two times, for a maximum maturity of three years.

Four Unique Requirements of the EWCP Loan
1) An applicant must submit cash flow projections to support the need for the loan and the ability to repay.
2) After the loan is made, the loan recipient must submit continual progress reports. SBA does not prescribe the Lender's fees.
3) SBA does not prescribe the interest rate for the EWCP.
4) SBA guarantees up to ninety (90) percent of an EWCP loan amount up to $1.5 million.

Guaranty Percents
For those applicants that meet the SBA's credit and eligibility standards, the Agency can guaranty up to ninety (90%) percent of loans (generally up to a maximum guaranty amount of $1.5 million).

Export Working Capital Program Loans (EWCP) Collateral A borrower must give SBA a first security interest equal to 100% of the EWCP guaranty amount. Collateral must be located in the United States

SBA Export Express combines the SBA's small business lending assistance with its technical assistance programs to help small businesses that have traditionally had difficulty in obtaining adequate export financing. The pilot program is available throughout the country and is expected to run through September 30, 2005.

SBA Export Express helps small businesses that have exporting potential, but need funds to buy or produce goods, and/or to provide services, for export.

Loan proceeds may be used to finance export development activities such as:
Participation in a foreign trade show;
Translation of product brochures or catalogues for use in overseas markets;
General lines of credit for export purposes;
Service contracts from buyers located outside the United States;
Transaction-specific financing needs associated with completing actual export orders; and/or
Purchase of real estate and equipment to be used in production of goods or services which will be expansion.
Provide term loans and other financing to enable small business concerns, including export trading companies and export management companies, to develop foreign markets;
Acquire, construct, renovate, modernize, improve or expand productive facilities or equipment to be used in the United States in the production of goods or services involved in international trade.

Who Can Use this Program?

SBA Export Express loans are available to persons who meet the normal requirements for an SBA business loan guaranty. Loan applicants must also demonstrate that the loan proceeds will enable them to enter a new export market or expand an existing export market, and- have been in business operation, though not necessarily in exporting, for at least 12 months.

How Does the Program Work?

Any lender that is authorized to participate in the SBA Express loan program may participate in SBA Export Express. SBA Export Express lenders use streamlined and expedited loan review and approval procedures to process SBA guaranteed loans. The lender uses its own loan analyses, loan procedures and loan documentation. Completed loan applications are submitted for approval to the SBA's processing center in Sacramento, California. The SBA provides the lender with a response, typically within 36 hours.

What is the SBA Guaranty

The SBA guaranty encourages lenders to make loans to small business exporters that they might not make on their own. The SBA's Export Express guaranty is 85 percent for loans up to $150,000 and 75 percent for loans more than $150,000 up to a maximum loan amount of $250,000. The maximum loan amount under Export Express is $250,000.

Terms, Interest Rates and Fees

Interest rates are negotiated between the borrower and the lender. Rates can either be fixed or variable, and are tied to the prime rate as published in The Wall Street Journal. Lenders may charge up to 6.5 percent over prime rate for loans of $50,000 or less and up to 4.5 percent over the prime rate for loans over $50,000.

Like most 7(a) loans, the maturity of an SBA Export Express term loan is usually five to 10 years for working capital, 10 to 15 years for machinery and equipment (not to exceed the useful life of the equipment), and up to 25 years for real estate. The maturity for revolving lines of credit may not exceed five years.

The guaranty and servicing fees under SBA Export Express are the same as for regular SBA 7(a) guaranty loans. (Link to Fees)

Technical Assistance
Because many small business exporters face unique problems and challenges, the SBA Export Express Program also includes technical assistance in the form of marketing, management and planning assistance.

Technical assistance is provided by SBA's U.S. Export Assistance Centers, in cooperation with SBA's network of resource partners, including the Small Business Development Centers (SBDCs) and Service Corps of Retired Executives (SCORE).

On approval of an SBA Export Express loan, a U.S. Export Assistance Center representative will contact the borrower to offer appropriate assistance. This assistance may include training offered through the SBA's Export Trade Assistance Partnership, SBDC International Trade Center, SCORE, District Export Council, or Export Legal Assistance Network.

What About My Other Financing Needs?
The SBA offers a range of long- and short-term financing options for small business exporters including the Export Working Capital Program (EWCP) and the International Trade loans. Information on both of these loans can be foundby selecting the link in the left hand column.

For more information about SBA Export Express or other SBA export assistance programs, please contact the SBA representative in the U.S. Export Assistance Center nearest you.

The Export Revolving Line provides funds for the manufacture or purchase of goods or services for export purposes or to penetrate foreign markets. This loan has a revolving feature, in that multiple lines of credit may exist simultaneously as long as they do not exceed $750,000 together. One qualification is that the firm applying for the loan must have been in business for a period of 12 months prior to the loan application date.

Handicapped Assistance Loans

The SBA also offers a number of direct loans for which it directly disburses funds. These loans are available to handicapped individuals and public or private nonprofit sheltered workshops.

First is the handicapped assistance loan, known as the HAL. There are two types of HAL loans: HAL-1 provides financial assistance to public or private nonprofit sheltered workshops; and HAL-2 provides financial assistance for small businesses owned 100percent by a handicapped person. The handicapped individual must actively participate in managing the business; businesses owned by an absentee handicapped owner are not eligible.

The interest rate on both of these loans is 3% and the maximum amount of the loan is limited to $150,000.

Vietnam-Era and Disabled Veteran programs

Another SBA direct loan program provides financial assistance for Vietnam-era and disabled veterans. Private financing and guaranty loans must be used if available. In order to qualify, at least 51 percent of the business must be owned by a qualifying veteran or veterans.

These loans have a maximum ceiling or loan amount of $150,000. To be eligible, Vietnam-era veterans must have served for more than 180 days between August 5, 1964 and May 7, 1975 and must not have received a dishonorable discharge. Veterans with 30 percent or more compensable disability or who have received a disability discharge are considered disabled veterans.

Collateral requirements are not nearly as strict for these programs as for other SBA loans. The SBA must be satisfied that loans are of sufficiently sound value or reasonably secured to ensure repayment. A side benefit of the SBA involvement with veterans is that they will provide special assistance and training as it applies to their specific business. This training is done in conjunction with a lender, if one is available.

Development Company Loan Program

This program operates in two different areas. One is the Local Development Company or 502 program. This type of loan is made to a local development company consisting of at least 25 stockholders. The loan is made by a participating bank and guaranteed by the SBA. For more information on local development companies, see Chapter 7. The other is the Certified Development Company loan, or 504 program. The purpose of this program is to help communities stimulate the growth and expansion of small businesses within a defined area of operation.

- Proceeds of Certified Development Company loans may be used for:
- Purchasing of existing buildings
- Purchasing land and land improvements
- Construction
- Purchasing machinery and equipment
- Paying interest on interim financing
- Financing a construction contingency fund, which cannot exceed 10 percent of the total construction costs
- Paying professional fees directly attributable to the project such as architectural, legal and accounting fees.

Although loans under the certified development program are for communities and community agencies, individuals and small businesses benefit from such loans by applying through local development companies, discussed in Chapter 9.

SBA programs are subject to change not only as to requirements for participants but to the availability of funds, actions of Congress and the SBA Administrator, and the state of the economy. For updated information on current and existing loan programs, contact your nearest SBA office or their web site at www.sba.gov.

Which of the many sources of money for entrepreneurs will be the best for your depends on your needs and objectives. In the next chapter we'll talk about your attitudes about money, and offer some pointers on what you have to do to get financing.

Defence Loan and Technical Assistance (DELTA) Program

SBA's Defense Economic Transition Assistance program is designed to help eligible small business contractors to transition from defense to civilian markets.

A small business is eligible if it has been detrimentally impacted by the closure (or substantial reduction) of a Department of Defense (DoD) installation, or the termination (or substantial reduction) of a Department of Defense Program on which the small business was a prime contractor, subcontractor, or supplier at any tier. In addition a business can be deemed eligible if it is located in community that has been detrimentally impacted by these same actions.

The DELTA program provides financial and technical assistance to defense-dependent small businesses which have been adversely affected by defense reductions. The goal of the program is to assist these businesses to diversify into the commercial market while remaining part of the defense industrial base. Complete information on eligibility and other rules is available from each SBA district office.

This program can be used in conjunction with both SBA's 7(a) and 504 Loan Programs and generally follows the provisions of each program. In order to be eligible for this program, small businesses must derive at least 25 percent of its revenues from Department of Defense or defense-related Department of Energy contracts or subcontracts in support of defense prime contracts in any one of five prior operating years.

Small businesses interested in utilizing this program must also meet at least one of the program's policy objectives:

- Job retention --- retains defense employees

- Job creation --- creates job opportunities and new economic activities in impacted communities

- Plant retooling and expansion ---modernizes or expands the plant and enables it to remain available to the Department of Defense.

U.S. Community Adjustment And Investment Program (CAIP)

General Description

CAIP is a program established to assist U.S. companies that are doing business in areas of the country that have been negatively affected by NAFTA. Funds administered by Treasury (see below) allow for the payment of fees on eligible loans. These fees include the 7(a) program guarantee fee (and subsidy) and the 504 program guarantee, CDC and lender fees. Depending on the loan size, the fees can be sizeable.

The CAIP works with the SBA in both their 7(a) Loan Guarantee Program and 504 Program to reduce borrower costs and increase the availability of these proven business assistance programs. CAIP can be used with both the 7(a) and 504 Loan Programs

Eligibility

To be eligible, certain criteria must be met; for example, the business must reside in a county noted as being negatively affected by NAFTA, based on job losses and the unemployment rate of the county; this was recently expanded to allow for granting eligibility to defined areas within a county (which will allow SBA to react quickly in offering to provide assistance when, for example, a plant closes).

In addition, there is a job creation component. For 7(a) loans, one job has to be created for every $70,000 SBA guarantees. For 504 loans, one job has to be created for every $50,000 SBA guarantees.

Eligible CAIP Communities

Currently, over 230 counties in 29 states are designated as eligible. Here is a listing of all communities (PDF File)which have been designated as eligible for funding under the Community Adjustment and Investment Program (CAIP). This second file contains the eligible zip codes for urban communities.

The objective of this program is to provide financial assistance to Employee Stock Ownership Plans. The employee trust must be part of a plan sponsored by the employer company and qualified under regulations set by either the Internal Revenue Service Code (as an Employee Stock Ownership Plan or ESOP) or the Department of Labor (the Employee Retirement Income Security Act or ERISA). Applicants covered by the ERISA regulations must also secure an exemption from the Department of Labor regulations prohibiting certain loan transactions.

Loan Amounts Available for Qualified Employee Trusts Loans

Effective December 22, 2000, a maximum loan amount of $2 million has been established for 7(a) loans. However, the maximum dollar amount the SBA can guaranty is generally $1 million. Small loans carry a maximum guaranty of 85 percent. Loans are considered small if the gross loan amount is $150,000 or less. For loans greater than $150,000, the maximum guaranty is 75 percent.

Who is Eligible for a Qualified Employee Trusts Loan?

SBA can assist qualified employee trusts that meet the requirements and conditions for an Employee Stock Ownership Plan (ESOP) as prescribed in all applicable IRS, Treasury, and Department of Labor regulations. The small business must provide all the funds needed to collaterize and repay the loan. A qualified employee trust may:

- re-lend proceeds to the employer by purchasing qualified employer securities, or
- purchase a controlling interest in the employer.

HUBZone

SBA's HUBZone program is in line with the efforts of both the Administration and Congress to promote economic development and employment growth in distressed areas by providing access to more Federal contracting opportunities. To be eligible for the program, a concern must meet all of the following criteria:

it must be a small business by SBA standards

it must be located in a "historically underutilized business zone(HUBZone),

it must be wholly owned and controlled by person(s) who are U.S. Citizens,

at least 35% of its employees must reside in a HUBZone.

Click here for more information about SBA's HUBZone program

8(a)/SDB (Small Disadvantaged Business)

To do business with the Federal government and to be certified under the 8(a) Program or as an SDB, you must register in the Central Contractor Registration (CCR) database, and complete the Small Business Supplemental Page within CCR. As a government-wide single point of vendor registration, CCR is a key aspect of streamlining and integrating electronic commerce into the Federal procurement process. Effective October 1, 2003, Federal Acquisition Regulation require contractors to register in CCR prior to award of any contract, basic agreement, basic ordering agreement, or blanket purchase agreement. It's easy to register in CCR. Just go to www.ccr.gov and select the "Start a New Registration" button.

Click here for more information about 8(a)/SDB programs

Chapter 11

How to Present Your Plan

All your documents are in shape, you've decided on the right bank and are dealing with the right loan officer. Now is the time to set up a presentation.

Generally, you will be making your presentation one-on-one to a lending officer, proving to him or her that you are credit worthy and the bank's money will be safe with you, thus enlisting his or her support of your loan application when it arrives at the bank's loan committee.

Sometimes, however, you will have to present your loan proposal to a group of investors. This chapter will show you how to make effective presentations to these larger audiences.

FOUR STEPS TO EFFECTIVE PRESENTATIONS

Presenting spoken information is different from writing it. An effective presentation includes four items: the opening, the preview, the major points, and the closing.

Opening

In speaking, your opening is even more important than in writing. You must immediately capture your listeners' interest while you establish your qualifications. An attention-grabbing opening stimulates your listeners' curiosity so they will look forward to what you'll tell them in the course of your presentation. A good opening could include an interesting sidelight about your business or yourself, an important statistic or a pertinent story.

Preview

The preview is useful because listeners, unlike readers, cannot skim over the general outline of your presentation. Your preview will tell them, in general terms, just what they can expect to learn or what you want them to do as a result of your presentation. List your three to five main points; listeners always remember better if they hear an overview at the beginning of your talk.

Major Points

In the main part of your presentation it's important to make your major points clearly. Don't expect your audience to know as much as you do about the subject you're covering. Limit your main points, emphasize when you are changing to a new subject and repeat your important points. Listeners cannot accept as much information as readers can and do not usually remember information they hear only once.

Closing

Your audience is probably going to remember your last statements. For your closing, avoid saying things like, "Well, that's about it," or "That's all I have to say." Move into your closing with a strong phrase such as "to summarize" or "in conclusion," and then restate your major points to reinforce the message.

VISUAL AIDS

Most people speak at about 100 words a minute, but can understand 400 to 1,000 words per minute. No matter how terrific you may be at presenting information, It's easy for the audience's attention to drift. A good way to keep listeners involved is to give them something visual to keep them concentrating on your ideas.

Visual aids range in type from printed materials to flip charts, to a full computer visual presentation. Decide which best meets your needs, based on the situation and your personal preferences. You can always combine various kinds of visual aids when they're called for.

In some situations you'll be limited to the simplest props; an agenda at the beginning of your presentation or a printed handout at the end. One excellent technique for involving an audience is to write down points as you make them; on a blank flipchart or overhead transparency. Use this method only if you feel comfortable with it. Nothing is worse than giving your listeners the sense that you are not fully in control of your information or materials.

Another way to use flip charts or overhead transparencies is to have them prepared with an outline of your information that you can point to during the presentation. As an added twist, you can leave blanks to fill in at the appropriate time or to even cross out some items and write over them to make your points more dramatically.

The most professional visual aids are those you create and package before the presentation. Professionally prepared flip charts, wall cards, charts, or computer graphic shows provide excellent support for a smooth performance.

Tips for Using Graphics

Once you have decided on the techniques to use you are ready to create your aids. Here are some rules you should follow to gain the most effectiveness:

- Use visual aids only if they explain your points better than you could by just speaking them. Remember, you're the star; your visual aids are the supporting players.
- Keep it simple. Trim your notes to key words and phrases. Don't write complete sentences. Reduce graphs to a minimum of detail.
- Keep it easy to read. Use large, clear, bold, well-spaced lettering and graphs. Don't include more than ten lines per page or slide.
- If you use colors to brighten and help clarify your message, be consistent. For example, use one color for major points and another for minor items or one color for ideas and another for financial matters. Dark blues, blacks, reds, and greens are best for type and graphs. Yellows and oranges are good for backgrounds. Save your darkest, highest contrast color for your most important point.
- Make each slide or page a completely self contained unit.
- Always provide a heading.
- Avoid passive statements, use the active voice always:
  Not: "The financial review should be issued by May 1."
  Better: "Review performance of all departments will be ready by May 1."
- Emphasize main ideas, do not bury them.

149

- Group similar ideas together.
- The best way to demonstrate relationships clearly is with a chart or graphs

FINAL PREPARATIONS

Even expert public speakers need memory aids to ensure that they cover all points. The best method is to copy an outline of your talk to 5 x 7 or 4 x 6 cards. These cards are easy to hold and allow you to add, subtract or rearrange your material easily. These cards are to be used for notes only. Do not write your presentation on them word-for-word; that would make you a reader, not a speaker. Each card should contain about five minutes' worth of material, printed large enough for you to see easily.

Once you have organized your presentation and prepared any visual aids you may need, it's time to practice your presentation. Practice will help you increase your self-confidence and improve your wording, identify any flaws in your speech and make sure your visual aids work smoothly with the content of your presentation.

Rehearse out loud, standing up, and use your visual aids just as you will in the actual presentation. It might help to rehearse in front of a mirror or record it on an audiotape or videotape so you can review your performance. Give your talk to a friend and get his or her suggestions. At this point, you want to improve your vocal expression and enthusiasm, and make your delivery as clear as possible.

The object is not to memorize the exact words or read your speech. It is a good idea, however, to memorize the opening and closing of your presentation. This will help you establish eye contact with your audience members when it's most crucial to gain their interest, support and approval.

Most important, keep cool. If you know your material and you've done your homework you should be ready for any audience. Be confident. Winston Churchill, one of the world's great speakers, said that when he felt anxious before a speech he would stop for a moment and reassured himself with the thought, "Look at those cabbage heads. They're just people, I have nothing to fear from them."

Chapter 12

The Bottom Line

P. T. Barnum, who certainly knew how to make money, said it over a century ago: "Money is a terrible master but an excellent servant." Truly these are words to live by. With this in mind, let's review the 11 guidelines for finding money for your small business.

ELEVEN GUIDELINES FOR FINDING MONEY FOR YOUR SMALL BUSINESS

1. Money is simply a tool that helps your business reach its goals. Not borrowing money when you need it is as bad as borrowing too much money that you can't repay.
2. By asking for a loan, you are really asking a lender to be your business partner.
3. Lenders are in business of making loans.
4. Lenders will only lend money they expect will be paid back and be profitable for them.

5. It's your responsibility to convince the lender that your business can and will pay back its loan.
6. Financial planning is basically about using your common sense in forecasting what is going to happen in your business.
7. Too many entrepreneurs start or operate their business with less money than they will really need.
8. Cash Flow or pro forma projections can help you see problems coming while there is still enough time to do something about them.
9. Writing a business plan forces you to think enough about every aspect of how the business is to operate to be able to discuss them with an investor or lender.
10. Establishing an ongoing business relationship is just as important as getting financing. You never know when you'll have to go back to the well for more money.
11. Every loan application is a new beginning.

Money Is a Tool

Money means a lot of different things to people, but the only way a serious businessperson can make the most of money is to understand that it is simply a tool that helps your business reach its goals. Not borrowing money when you need it, and can repay it, is as bad as borrowing too much money that can't be repaid.

You're Really Looking For a Partner

When you approach a lender you are asking him or her to be your business partner. The money he or she lends you is an investment in your ideas, your business ability and your dependability as a person.

Lending Money Is the Lender's Business

Remember, lenders are in the business of making loans, and they are always out to make the best loan record they can. They will only lend money they anticipate will be paid back and be profitable for them. Unlike family members or friends, their interest is strictly business, so they have to be careful about the people and companies to whom they lend money and how they do it. Remember, a bank must make 97 good loans to make up for one bad loan.

You Must Sell the Lender on Your Business

It's your responsibility to convince the lender that your business is one that can and will pay back its loan. Before you go looking for a loan, make sure that you have done all the planning and preparation. A good loan proposal must persuade a lender that it is in his or her interest to lend you money.

You will have to show the lender how the business is going to repay the loan. To do that, you have to prepare a financial plan as evidence that you know what you are doing and how you are preparing for success. You have to demonstrate that you've thought through as many of the business problems that you can foresee. In a way, you have to sell others on your dream - and in order to persuade them to part with their cash, you have to convince them that you are worth the investment.

Make Sure Your Company is Adequately Capitalized

A new or established business needs enough money to:

- Buy the equipment, tools, raw materials, inventory or whatever else it takes to build the products or provide the service it sells; and
- Pay the day-to-day operating expenses until the profits begin or are large enough to cover all expenses.

154

Most businesses that fail, do so because they were undercapitalized; they didn't have, or were unable to get, enough money to pay their bills. In most cases this occurs due to poor planning. Too many entrepreneurs start their businesses, or work day to day, with less money than they really need, assuming everything will work out the way they want it to. And when their company hits a rough spot, this poor planning can lead to an unnecessary business failure.

Doing It Right: The Four Basic Steps

Financial planning is basically about looking ahead and forecasting what is going to happen in your business, and then using your common sense! There are four basic steps you must take in preparing a financial plan: prepare a cash flow projection, a business plan and a loan proposal, and then explore potential sources of capital.

The Cash Flow Projection. In previous chapters, we discussed what goes into a cash flow or pro forma projection. This excellent planning tool can help you visualize the future. By projecting what you think you are going to sell and spend during the upcoming months, you can foresee problems coming while there is still enough time to do something about them.

The Business Plan Basically, the business plan answers the following questions:
1. What is the business?
2. Which will be the most profitable products?
3. What are the major markets and competitors?

It also presents the budget and cash flow projections for at least the next 12 months.

Writing a business plan forces you to think enough about each of the aspects of how the business is to operate, so that you can discuss them with an investor or

155

lender. The business plan is important because it tells the investor or lender that you have thoroughly charted your business. It is designed to give them confidence in you.

The Loan Proposal The loan proposal is required for all but the most informal financing arrangements. It offers the best way to get your story out to a lot of people quickly and professionally as you shop for money. Think of your loan proposal as a mini-business plan that can easily be customized to show each prospective lender or investor the information that is needed or requested.

Your proposal must fit your needs, wants and background. It must also fit the needs and interests of the investor or lender to whom you are applying for financing.

Potential Sources of Capital After you have done your basic planning and have prepared your loan proposal, you can start looking for the best source for the amount of money you need.

Where you get your money is largely dependent upon how much you need. Various sources are comfortable with different amounts. Generally, the more money you want, the more "packaging" you need and the more lengthy your written proposal.

Have a Realistic Attitude

Remember, the golden rule in business is, he or she who has the gold makes the rules. If you go into the money market with unrealistic attitudes about money and the people who lend it, you're in for some disappointments and frustration. The only practical way to obtain financing is to view the process objectively. This is a business arrangement, pure and simple.

Invest in Your Own Idea

Lenders want to see if you believe in your company enough to risk all or part of your personal assets. They could decide that if you don't have enough confidence to guarantee the debt, you should not be borrowing the money.

Don't Burn Your Bridges

Getting financing is important, but establishing an ongoing business relationship is just as important. You never know when you'll have to go back to the well for more money. Being truthful with the lender, repaying your loans and fulfilling all your commitments will help to establish your business credit rating not only with your initial lender but for any financial dealings you'll have in the years to come.

Every Loan Application Is A New Beginning

A loan refusal is only one lender's judgment of the uncertainty involved in that loan request. It is not an evaluation of your worth as a person.

Even if your first plan doesn't pan out, you'll soon get better at forecasting with experience. Every newly approached lender gives you a fresh opportunity to make your case better. Learn the lessons or your previous rejections and determine not to repeat them.

Money Is the Key to Success in Business

Our hope and intention, with this book, is to give you the necessary information and background to make finding money sources and getting funding for your ideas as painless as possible. As with everything else in life, the better you follow the lessons of the practices we've presented and prepare for your day with the lenders the more successful you will be.

INDEX